PLATO

Parmenides

For Adolf,
with admiration
and affection,
MaryLouise

PLATO

Parmenides

Translated by
MARY LOUISE GILL and PAUL RYAN

Introduction by
MARY LOUISE GILL

Hackett Publishing Company, Inc.
Indianapolis/Cambridge

Plato: ca. 428–347 B.C.

Copyright 1996 by Hackett Publishing Company, Inc.

Printed in the United States of America

00 99 98 97 96   1 2 3 4 5

For further information, please address

Hackett Publishing Company, Inc.
P.O. Box 44937
Indianapolis, Indiana 46244-0937

Cover design by Listenberger & Associates

Text design by Dan Kirklin

Library of Congress Cataloging-in-Publication Data

Plato
      [Parmenides. English]
      Parmenides/Plato; translated by Mary Louise Gill and Paul Ryan;
introduction by Mary Louise Gill.
           p.   cm.
      Includes bibliographical references.
      ISBN 0-87220-329-8 (alk. paper)   ISBN 0-87220-328-X (pbk.: alk.
paper)
      1. Socrates. 2. Parmenides. 3. Ontology. 4. Zeno of Elea.
5. Reasoning—Early works to 1800. 6. Dialectic—Early works to
1800. I. Gill, Mary Louise, 1950– . II. Ryan, Paul, 1929– .
III. Title.
B378.A5G5513   1996
184—dc20   95-48981
                                                                 CIP

The paper used in this publication meets the minimum requirements
of American National Standard for Information Sciences—Perma-
nence of Paper for Printed Library Materials, ANSI Z39.48-1984.

∞

Contents

Preface

Plato's *Parmenides* is a difficult dialogue, and for that reason the introduction to the translation is quite extensive. The aim has been to give the reader as much assistance as possible. Although a translation is already an interpretation, Paul Ryan and I have tried to keep interpretive intrusion to a minimum in the notes to the translation. Most of our notes either indicate places where we have diverged from Burnet in his Oxford edition of the Greek text, or present an alternative translation that we have rejected. Defense of our interpretive choices is given in the introduction.

We thank John Cooper for much valuable advice on the translation and for ensuring that we thought carefully about our philological and philosophical reasons for decisions in the translation.

As for the introduction, I have incurred many debts. I particularly thank Paul Coppock for suggesting the project in the first place, for reading two drafts and giving me acute philosophical criticisms, and for clarifying my understanding of many questions relevant to the project. I am grateful to Myles Burnyeat for strategic advice at the outset and for valuable criticisms on a draft of the manuscript. Three readers who have worked extensively on the *Parmenides* gave me detailed written comments on the entire manuscript. Malcolm Schofield was an astute critic, and all of his objections, to the extent that I have succeeded in answering them, have resulted in improvements. Verity Harte gave me many ideas for the interpretation of the dialogue, and the introduction is much better for her insights. Patricia Curd, who read the manuscript for Hackett, gave me advice that resulted in some significant changes. I am very grateful to Paul Ryan, my co-translator, who read the introduction on three occasions and suggested ways to improve it. More important, in the three years that we worked together on the translation, he taught me a great deal about the Greek language and Plato's use of it in the *Parmenides*.

Several other people have read the whole or a substantial part of the introduction and have given me helpful comments: Edwin

Allaire, Thomas Chance, John Malcolm, John Newell, Katherine Nolan, and Michael Wedin. For help on particular points, I also thank Rogers Albritton, Harry Avery, Alan Bowen, Judith Cross, Patrick Findler, James Lennox, Henry Mendell, Andrew Miller, David Sedley, Hans-Peter Stahl, and Robert Wardy. My work on the *Parmenides* has profited from the opportunity to present it at different stages in a number of forums. I gave three graduate seminars on the dialogue: at the University of Pittsburgh (1992), at UCLA (1994), and at the University of California at Davis (1995). In 1994 I gave a paper on the first regress argument in the *Parmenides* at the University of California at Berkeley and Davis, at the University of New Mexico, at Claremont Graduate School, at Eötvös University in Budapest, Hungary, and at the "B" Club, Cambridge University. In 1995 I gave a paper on the functions of being in Part II of the *Parmenides* at the University of Rochester. I am grateful to those audiences for their questions, which kept me rethinking the issues.

My acknowledgments would be incomplete without mentioning G.E.L. Owen, who inspired a generation of students to continue his persistent exploration of the *Parmenides*. My work on the dialogue owes much to him.

Mary Louise Gill

Introduction

The *Parmenides* is one of Plato's most important dialogues and without doubt his most enigmatic. In works like the *Phaedo* and the *Republic*, Plato's Socrates speaks of entities known as forms. Forms are eternal, unchanging objects, each with a unique nature, which we grasp with our minds but not with our senses. Forms are supposed to explain the properties things have in our changing world. For instance, the form of beauty, which is eternally and unqualifiedly beautiful, is supposed to explain the beauty of things we experience in the world around us. But the *Phaedo* and the *Republic* raise more questions than they answer. Neither dialogue gives a systematic account of forms but simply appeals to them in the course of treating other topics, such as the immortality of the soul (*Phaedo*) or the education of the philosopher-king (*Republic*). The *Parmenides* is the only dialogue that sets out a theory of forms as the explicit focus of its attention. So we turn to this dialogue in expectation that it will enable us to understand Plato's most famous contribution to the history of philosophy.

In the first part of the *Parmenides*, Plato has Socrates, as a youth, set out a theory of forms, which is then subjected to intense and sustained scrutiny by the master-philosopher Parmenides. The theory appears to fare rather badly when put to the test, and by the end of the examination we might think that it should be abandoned. What are we to make of this apparent failure? Are the objections answerable, and is Socrates simply too inexperienced to answer them? Or did Plato regard the objections as fatal to his own previous views? Is the *Parmenides* the honest assessment of a philosopher of heroic stature who both recognized and publicly confessed that his own greatest philosophical achievement was seriously flawed, and who did not know how to put matters right? Or did he think the objections were answerable but only by substantially revising his views? Does the *Parmenides* mark a turning point in Plato's philosophy, recording a crucial stage of reflection and self–criticism after his self-assured masterpiece, the *Republic*? If so, where should we look for his revisions? Should we look for his answers in dialogues like the *Theaetetus, Sophist, Statesman,* and *Philebus,* which most scholars date after the *Parmenides*?[1] Or should we look for his answers in the long second part of the *Parmenides* itself? These questions indicate why the *Parmenides* is pivotal for understanding Plato's philosophy more generally. The fact that there is no general agreement about the answers is one reason why the dialogue continues to puzzle and fascinate its readers.

Even if we consider the *Parmenides* on its own, apart from its relation to other Platonic works, the dialogue is an enigma. After a brief introductory section (126a–127a) which raises its own interpretive problems, the dialogue breaks into two unequal and seemingly self-contained parts (127a–134e and 137c–166c), with a short transitional section connecting the two (134e–137c). Part I, which is lively and conversational, contains a discussion of Zeno's book, Socrates' proposal about forms, and Parmenides' criticisms of Socrates' proposal. In the transitional section, after Socrates has failed to rescue his theory, Parmenides surprises us by saying that there must be forms if we are to have anywhere to turn our thought and if we are to preserve the power of dialectic. Socrates' problem, Parmenides says, is that he has posited forms too soon, before he has been properly trained.

Part II, which takes up three-quarters of the dialogue, gives a lengthy demonstration of the sort of training Parmenides has in mind. Although the pattern of question and answer is preserved in Part II, the answerer makes no positive contributions to the discussion, as Socrates did in Part I, but simply agrees or asks for clarification. Part II, though it breaks up into a series of deductions, is one long, relentless stretch of argument, lacking

---

1. A further question concerns Plato's *Timaeus*, traditionally regarded as a late dialogue, which appears consistent with the *Phaedo* and *Republic* in its treatment of forms. Does it ignore the objections in the *Parmenides* and so indicate that those objections were not seriously intended or not regarded as serious? Or are scholars wrong to date the *Timaeus* after the *Parmenides*? Is the *Timaeus* the crowning work of Plato's so-called middle period, before he recognized that his views about forms required substantial rethinking? Or does its treatment of forms avoid, or perhaps even answer, the objections raised in the *Parmenides*?

the social interactions and play of character that brighten Part I. Both its form and its content are so difficult to fathom that some scholars have suggested that Plato could not have meant it seriously. Others have read it with the utmost seriousness, some finding in it a magnificent metaphysical system, others a treasure-house of philosophical puzzles.

It has been suggested, on grounds of the difference in style between the two parts, that Plato wrote them at separate times and patched them together in the transitional section.[2] This view and the observation that the two parts seem to stand on their own have encouraged the belief that the parts can be tackled separately and that Part I can be understood without Part II. Classes on Plato often assign only Part I, which is a good deal more accessible than Part II and more obviously relevant to our understanding of Plato's metaphysics. One aim of this introduction is to show that the *Parmenides* is a unified dialogue and that a proper understanding of Part I depends on working through the exercise that constitutes Part II.

This introduction should preferably not be read in its entirety before the dialogue itself is read. Since the introduction follows Plato's organization, each section of the introduction can be read in conjunction with the corresponding section of the dialogue.

The Frames (126a–127a)

The *Parmenides* records a conversation between Socrates as a youth and Parmenides and Zeno, distinguished philosophers visiting Athens from Elea. The conversation is staged many years before the dramatic date of its being reported to us. Our narrator, Cephalus of Clazomenae, has come to Athens with some friends. They meet Adeimantus and Glaucon in the marketplace and ask to see Antiphon, who reportedly heard the conversation in his youth from Pythodorus and memorized it. The conversation is thus reported to us within three frames—we get it from Cephalus, who got it from Antiphon, who got it from Pythodorus,

2. See Ryle's "Afterword" to his 1939 paper in Allen (ed.) 1965. In the notes modern works are cited by author and date, works by Plato by title, and other ancient or early modern works by author and title. Full citations are given in the Bibliography.

who heard it himself. Why does Plato use this elaborate framing device?

One reason for the three-tiered frame is doubtless to indicate that the reported conversation is remote in time. Parmenides is represented as being about sixty-five years old, Zeno about forty, and Socrates as very young. Since Socrates died in 399 B.C. at age seventy, he was born in 469. We are told that Parmenides and Zeno visited Athens for the Great Panathenaea, a festival held in honor of Athens' patron goddess Athena. Although a festival honored her every year, that of the Great Panathenaea was celebrated on a grander scale once every four years. Given Socrates' claimed youth, the dramatic date of Parmenides' and Zeno's visit is taken to coincide with the Great Panathenaea in 450 B.C., when Socrates was eighteen or nineteen. Had Cephalus visited Athens before the year of Socrates' trial and execution in 399, he would surely have gone to Socrates himself to learn the details of that discussion. Since he and his friends do not seek out Socrates or anyone else who was present on the earlier occasion, we have reason to set the dramatic date of the reporting after 399, and thus more than fifty years after the event, by which time all those who took part in the discussion were presumably dead.

The framing device serves a further purpose. Although this is not the only Platonic dialogue narrated by someone who was not present at the event he reports, it is unusual in the complexity of its frame and in the fact that our narrator has not verified his account with anyone who took part in the conversation or who was an eyewitness (contrast Apollodorus, the narrator in the *Symposium*, who tells us he checked the details for accuracy with Socrates). By setting the dramatic date of the reporting long after the date of the event reported, when the accuracy of Cephalus' account can no longer be established, Plato allows us to question the historical accuracy of the conversation reported. Indeed, if we focus on the question of historicity, we are bound to ask ourselves whether Socrates, Parmenides, and Zeno ever had a conversation of the sort recounted.

In the *Theaetetus* (183e–184a) and again in the *Sophist* (217c), Plato has Socrates refer to the meeting he once had with Parmenides, when Parmenides was old and he was very young. Although these references could indicate that such a meeting actually took place, they may merely indicate that Plato wants his audience to read the *Theaetetus* and the *Sophist* against the philosophical background of the *Parmenides*. In the *Parmenides* Socrates expounds a theory of forms whose details remind us of the treatment of forms in the *Phaedo*, a dialogue that recounts the conversation Socrates had with friends on the last day of his life. Not only is it historically unlikely that Socrates would rely in old age on a theory that had been severely criticized fifty years earlier, it is also unlikely from what we know of Socrates' character (as represented in Plato's so-called Socratic dialogues— works like the *Apology*, *Euthyphro*, and *Crito*) that the historical Socrates would ever have held such a theory. Socrates, who notoriously claimed his ignorance, was not a man who was committed to theories. On the contrary, he subjected the views of others to cross-examination without endorsing a position himself.

In the *Parmenides* Plato reverses the characteristic role of Socrates and his interlocutor. Here Socrates is the person who advocates a position, and Parmenides is the one who subjects it to cross-examination. As in the *Phaedo* and the *Republic*, Plato uses the persona of Socrates in the *Parmenides* to expound views that he, as author, wants to introduce for discussion. They are not views attributable to the historical Socrates.[3] Plato alerts the reader to the possibility that the conversation in the *Parmenides* is fiction by using the triple frame and setting the dramatic date of the conversation far in the past, so that none of its details can be confirmed.

Another peculiarity of the introductory section is Plato's choice of narrators—Cephalus, Antiphon, and Pythodorus. Pythodorus was Parmenides' and Zeno's host. Though he contributes

---

3. We should also beware of assuming that Plato's own views coincide with those of one or another of the characters in his dialogues. In reading the *Parmenides* it is of course worth asking ourselves whether Plato is to be identified with the young Socrates who defends a theory of forms or with Parmenides who criticizes it, or whether Socrates represents his younger self, Parmenides his older self. But we should remain open to the possibility that Plato is examining forms and their functions from various perspectives without endorsing any of those perspectives himself.

nothing to the discussion, we are told that he rehearsed it after-
ward, thus giving Antiphon the opportunity to learn it by heart.
According to *Alcibiades* I (119a), Pythodorus paid Zeno one hun-
dred minae (a substantial sum) for instruction. This testimony
could indicate that Pythodorus had philosophical aspirations in
his youth or simply that he aimed to become a skilled political
debater. In later life he had a political and military career.[4] So
Plato's Athenian audience would probably remember him as a
politician, not as a philosopher.

Antiphon was Plato's half brother.[5] We are told in the *Parmenides* that he was half brother of Adeimantus and Glaucon by the
same mother; they were Plato's full brothers. (Adeimantus and
Glaucon, who figure in the opening scene of the *Parmenides*,
are Socrates' interlocutors in the *Republic*.) Though Antiphon
memorized the discussion in his youth and repeats it to Cephalus
and his friends upon request, the only significant detail we learn
about him in the *Parmenides* is that he now devotes most of his
time to horses. The visitors find him thus engaged, and some
cajoling is needed to get him to give the recitation. Whatever
philosophical aspirations Antiphon may once have had have by
now been replaced by one of the intellectually less demanding
pursuits of the upper class.

This dialogue is our sole evidence for Cephalus, who narrates
the conversation to an unspecified audience (and to us readers).
We do not know whether he is a historical person or a dramatic
fiction. He has come with some friends to Athens from Clazomenae in Ionia (native city of the fifth-century natural philosopher Anaxagoras) for the express purpose of hearing Antiphon
recite the conversation. He identifies his companions as keen
philosophers, and he too is apparently keen, since he repeats
this highly technical philosophical conversation to an audience.
Even so, his own style of speaking appears more colloquial than
philosophical (a fact that cannot be adequately captured in a

---

4. According to Thucydides, *History of the Peloponnesian War*, Pythodorus
served as a general in Sicily in 426–425 during the Peloponnesian War.
When he retreated, he was charged with bribery and banished from
Athens.

5. Plato's family tree is given by Kirchner 1901–1903.

translation).[6] Perhaps nothing significant turns on this point of Platonic artistry, but it does pique our curiosity as to why this person found this discussion worth reporting.[7] What are we to make of this odd group of individuals—a politician, a horse fancier, and someone from Ionia? Given the technical difficulty of the second part of the dialogue, it seems unlikely that Plato intended this work for the general public, which the three narrators might be taken to represent. Furthermore, in the transitional section to Part II, Parmenides and Zeno twice repeat that the upcoming demonstration is appropriate training only for the restricted few (136d, 137a). Perhaps Plato uses the chain of narrators—Cephalus, Antiphon, Pythodorus— to guide readers (such as ourselves) from outside the Platonic circle inward. Perhaps he also wants to alert his readers that the upcoming discussion of forms and the exercise in Part II have implications not just for members of the Platonic circle but for anyone who wants to gain insight into the truth.

PART I (127a–137c)

Parmenides and Zeno (127a–128e)

Seven people were present for the original conversation—Parmenides, Zeno, Socrates, Aristotle,[8] Pythodorus, and two unnamed others.

---

6. For instance, he has a penchant for starting his sentences with "And" and for colloquial use of inferential particles. Cephalus speaks in his own voice only in his statements and narrative in the introductory section, and in his later intrusions at 136d and 136e. Elsewhere he appears to be reporting the words of others verbatim, and the style is markedly different.

7. It may be a sheer coincidence (if anything in Plato can be attributed to that) that this narrator has a namesake in the first book of the *Republic*. That Cephalus was a rich old man who could scarcely be credited with intellectual gifts. The possible implications of this connection are discussed by Miller 1986, 18–25.

8. Not the great fourth-century philosopher, who was Plato's student. Aristotle in the *Parmenides* is a young comrade of Socrates' who later (404 B.C.) became one of the Thirty Tyrants in Athens at the end of the

Parmenides of Elea is the main speaker. After an opening exchange between Zeno and Socrates and a long speech by Socrates, Parmenides leads the rest of the discussion. Why does Plato choose Parmenides to play this dominant role? One reason is that the *Parmenides* explores an issue for which the historical Parmenides was famous. During the initial conversation between Socrates and Zeno, Socrates claims that Parmenides said in his poem that "the all is one" (128a–b). Although this statement has no explicit counterpart in the extant fragments of Parmenides, his argument implies that reality consists of just one thing.

The historical Parmenides wrote a philosophical poem in two parts, which—to judge from its serious reception by Plato and Aristotle in the fourth century, not to mention by natural philosophers such as Anaxagoras and Democritus in the fifth—evidently turned the philosophical world on its head. The first part of his poem, much of which is extant, expounds the "Way of Truth"; the second, which survives only in scattered fragments, presents the "Way of Mortal Opinions." Parmenides famously argued in his Truth that there are only two conceivable paths of inquiry. The first, which he advocates, is the path that "it is and cannot not be"; the second, which he rejects, is the path that "it is not and must not be" (DK 28 B2).[9] According to Parmenides, this second path cannot be taken, because we can neither know nor indicate what is not. Instead, ordinary people try to take a middle way, believing that "to be and not to be are the same and not the same" (DK 28 B6). This middle way is a path of contradictions. So the only true path is the first.

Many questions may be asked about the path that Parmenides advocates. We want to know what subject he is talking about when he says "it" is. In fact, he says simply "is" (*estin*), without explicitly mentioning a subject. Since Greek is an inflected language (i.e., the form of a word indicates its function in a sentence), a verb alone can serve as a complete sentence, and a

---

Peloponnesian War. He is Parmenides' respondent in the second part of the dialogue.

9. References to fragments of Parmenides and Zeno are cited from the standard edition of Diels and Kranz 1951 (referred to in the text as "DK"). For translation and discussion of the fragments of these philosophers, see Kirk, Raven, and Schofield 1983 or McKirahan 1994.

subject is understood from the context. Here no subject is easily supplied, so we are bound to ask "*What* is?" Later in the poem he refers to the subject as "what is" (*to eon*), which doesn't help very much. Perhaps he has in mind any subject of discourse, or perhaps from the start he is talking about one subject in particular. We also want to know what he means when he says it "is." The Greek verb "to be" can be construed in various ways in English, depending on whether the verb completes the sentence (as in "the sea is") or has a further completion (as in "the sea is blue" or "a horse is an animal"). There is no separate verb "exists" in classical Greek, but when the verb "is" is used without a completion (as in "the sea is"), it can be translated into English as "exists." So Parmenides could be saying that the subject of his inquiry exists, indeed must exist. Since the verb "to be" can also operate as a copula, which links subject and predicate in a sentence (as in "the sea is blue"), his claim could be that his subject has, indeed must have, some character or other. The meaning of "is" in the two contexts strikes us as different, because we describe objects that do not exist (as in the sentence "Pegasus is a winged horse, but he doesn't exist").[10] Parmenides, however, may have supposed that "is" has the same meaning in both contexts. He may have thought that if something is (exists), then it is something or other. If that was his view, and we asked him about Pegasus, he would say: "Pegasus is, since he is describable." He would, however, immediately add: " 'Pegasus' is a mere name that you mortals use in talking about what is" (cf. DK 28 B8.38–41).

Even if at the outset Parmenides is talking about any subject of inquiry, his argument eventually makes clear that there is only one such subject.[11] There is just one thing, because we can neither distinguish anything from it nor differentiate parts within it. By means of a series of deductive proofs (the first of their kind in the history of philosophy), Parmenides argued that this

---

10. For a discussion of the uses of the verb "to be" in ancient Greek and why our intuitions about being and existence differ from those of the Greeks, see Kahn 1966, 1976, and 1986.

11. This claim has been disputed by Mourelatos 1970, 130–33, and Curd 1991.

object is ungenerated and indestructible, whole, uniform,[12] unchangeable, and complete (DK 28 B8). Parmenides' Truth thus challenges the evidence of our senses, which report a plurality of changing things.

In attributing some degree of reality to the changing objects of ordinary experience and in positing a plurality of intelligible forms, the Platonist rejects the Parmenidean position. Even so, to judge from the *Phaedo*, each form, though distinguished from others by its own proper character, shares with all forms what we may call the "formal" or "ideal" properties of Parmenidean being:[13] each is ungenerated and indestructible, unchangeable, intelligible, and uniform.[14] Each form is a stable entity with a unique nature.

The controlling issue of the *Parmenides* is the oneness attributed to forms. In Part I Parmenides will repeatedly show that despite Socrates' conviction that each form is one, it is after all many. One lesson of Part I is that oneness itself is slippery. What do we mean when we say that something is one? Do we mean that it is a single thing? Or that it is a whole composed of parts? What is oneness itself? This slippery notion is the subject of the exercise in Part II. So Plato chooses Parmenides as the main speaker in the *Parmenides* because he will use Parmenidean themes in his investigation of forms. Socrates' early mention of Parmenides' thesis, that "the all is one," sets the stage for the focus on oneness to follow.

Little is known about Zeno's life. We are told in the *Parmenides* that on the occasion of their visit he and Parmenides brought Zeno's book to Athens for the first time. According to Proclus in his

---

12. The meaning of *mounogenes* is disputed, though most scholars now agree that it is the word Parmenides used. Among other possible translations are "one of a kind," "unique," "of one kind." If "uniform" is right, the idea is that the object is the same through and through, not divisible into parts of different sorts.

13. These are properties a form has as a form, rather than as the particular form that it is.

14. Cf. *Symposium* 211a–d and *Phaedo* 80b with Parmenides fragment 8 (DK 28 B8). Plato uses the word *monoeides*, where Parmenides uses *mounogenes*. Plato speaks of the cosmos as *monogenes* at *Timaeus* 31b, and there the word presumably means "one of a kind" or "unique."

commentary on Plato's *Parmenides*, Zeno's book contained forty *logoi*, or arguments, each of which attacked the thesis that things are many by deriving contradictory consequences from it.[15] Zeno himself claims in our dialogue that he wrote the book as a young man in defense of Parmenides' argument against those who tried to make fun of it. The aim was to show that their hypothesis, that things are many, has consequences more absurd than those of Parmenides' hypothesis, that the all is one (128b–e).

The discussion in the *Parmenides* begins just after Zeno has completed a reading of his treatise. Socrates asks him to reread the first hypothesis of the first argument (127d). We are not told what specific arguments Zeno gave for his conclusions, but we are given the shape of the general argument: If things are many, they must be both like and unlike; this is impossible, because the same things cannot have incompatible properties. Therefore things are not many (127e). We are missing the arguments Zeno used to show that the same things, if many, are both like and unlike. Presumably Plato ignored them because the arguments Zeno actually used were immaterial.[16] What mattered for Plato's

---

15. Proclus, *Commentary on Plato's Parmenides* 694.23–25. Proclus was a Neoplatonist who lived in the fifth century A.D., and he may not have had access to Zeno's book. Since he was probably using a work by someone else who was supplying readers of the *Parmenides* with the other arguments Zeno read out on the occasion described in our dialogue, his claim is not reliable evidence for the historical Zeno. See Dillon's introduction to Proclus' commentary, pp. xxxviii–xliii.

16. We have one genuine fragment from Zeno's book that indicates the sort of arguments he used. Here the predicates are "limited" and "unlimited." Simplicius (sixth century A.D.) preserves the statement:

> In proving again that, if things are many, the same things are limited and unlimited, Zeno writes the following in his own words:
>
> "If things are many, they must be as many as they are, and neither more nor less than that. But if they are as many as they are, they would be limited.
>
> "If things are many, the things that are are unlimited; for there are always others between the things that are, and again others between those. And in this way the things that are are unlimited." (DK 29 B3)

The conclusion of this reductio, like the one described in the *Parmenides*, is that things are not many.

own purpose was the apparent contradiction that Zeno exposed—that the same things are both F and not-F (e.g., both like and unlike). Socrates introduces his theory of forms to resolve the contradiction.

Socrates' Long Speech (128e–130a)

We might well ask why anyone should be bothered by Zeno's contradictions. The same thing can of course be both F and not-F, if it is F in one respect or relation and not-F in another, or F at one time and not-F at another. For example, Simmias is both like and unlike Socrates; he is like Socrates in species (since both are human beings), but unlike him in size (since he is taller than Socrates). There is a contradiction only if the same thing is F and not-F at the same time, in the same respect and in relation to the same thing. Plato has Socrates state a version of the Law of Non-Contradiction in *Republic* IV, and the qualifiers are explicitly mentioned. Even so, the speakers in Plato's dialogues, though they quite regularly mention the qualifiers, nonetheless find it paradoxical that the same thing is both F and not-F, even if it is F and not-F in different respects or relations. Appeal to forms is felt to dissolve the paradox. Let us start by looking at the discussion in *Republic* IV, which sheds some light on the handling of contradictions in Plato's dialogues.

In *Republic* IV Socrates is arguing that the soul has three parts. He says:

> "It is clear that the same thing cannot act in opposite ways or be in opposite states at the same time, in the same respect and in relation to the same thing. So if we find these opposite actions and states occurring in their case [i.e., in the case of the parts of the soul], we shall know that they are not the same thing but more than one." (436b–c)

Why, if someone simultaneously wants and doesn't want the same thing, say a drink (439a–c), is this taken to show that the person's soul has more than one part—a part that wants the drink, and another that doesn't want it?

Consider some examples Socrates discusses. Suppose a man waves his arms while standing still. We are told that we ought not to say that the same man, at the same time, is both at rest and in motion. Instead we should say that part of him is at rest, and part in motion (436c–d). Again, suppose a top is twirling in the same place. We should not say that the top as a whole is both at rest and in motion, but attribute these opposites to different parts of it. Distinguishing the axis and the circumference of the top, we should say that the axis is at rest and the circumference in motion (436d–e). In these cases contradictions are dissolved by denying that the subject to which these opposites are ascribed is one thing. The subject that is F is different from the subject that is not-F. This solution seems plausible enough in the cases discussed in the *Republic*, where we can differentiate physical parts of a thing. Analogy with these cases also makes plausible the division of the soul into three parts to account for psychological conflicts.

But now consider an example in the *Phaedo*. Simmias is said to be both large and small—large in relation to Socrates, small in relation to Phaedo. In this case there seems to be just one object, Simmias himself, with a height of, say, five feet six inches; and this one object is large in relation to a smaller man, but small in relation to a larger man. We cannot distinguish distinct physical components as the subjects of the opposite features, as Socrates did in the *Republic*.

How can it be true that the same object is both large and small? We moderns see no difficulty, because we regard "large" and "small" as incomplete predicates and resolve the contradiction by adding the completions. Once we specify the individual or class of individuals in relation to which Simmias is large or small, the contradiction disappears. Simmias is large in relation to Socrates, small in relation to Phaedo; he is large for a light-weight boxer, small for a middle-weight boxer, and so on. Plato, however, seems to regard "large" and "small" as complete predicates—predicates that specify genuine properties an object has—and for that reason he finds the apparent contradiction troubling. So the statement "Simmias is large and small" seems as vexing as the statement "the same thing is round and square," because the properties are incompatible with each other.

The *Phaedo* presents a metaphysical theory to resolve the apparent contradiction. Socrates says that Simmias is large by partaking of the form of largeness, small by partaking of the form of smallness. By partaking of largeness he has largeness in him, and by partaking of smallness he has smallness in him. According to this account, it is not by being Simmias that Simmias is larger than Socrates. Nor is it by his determinate height that he is larger (since the very same height makes him small in another comparison). Instead, Simmias is larger than Socrates by the largeness he happens to have, and he is smaller than Phaedo by the smallness he happens to have (102c).

Let me introduce a piece of terminology which will also be used in discussing the *Parmenides*. I shall use the label "immanent character" to designate features of objects that forms are invoked to explain. Features like largeness and smallness, which Socrates designates in the *Phaedo* as "in us," will be called "immanent characters."[17] The label will be applied to only some of an object's features, since only some are explained by appeal to forms. In the *Phaedo* Simmias' largeness and smallness are immanent characters, but not his height of five feet six inches, the ruddiness of his complexion, or his being a human being.[18] Use of the label need not commit us to a view about what sort of entities immanent characters are. As we shall see, different interpretations of their ontological status are appropriate in different contexts.[19]

How does Socrates' solution in the *Phaedo* work? Apparently the statement "Simmias is large and small" can be true, because Simmias partakes of the opposite forms largeness and smallness, and so has two immanent characters, largeness and smallness. How does this proposal eliminate the paradox of

---

17. "Immanent" simply means "present in" a subject.

18. Should Plato in some other context invoke forms to explain these features, they can then be labeled immanent characters. For instance, the question is raised in the *Parmenides* whether there is a form of human being. If there is such a form, the feature it explains can be called an immanent character.

19. Whether immanent characters are forms as participated in, or parts of forms, or instances of forms, or somehow correspond to forms depends on, among other things, the status of forms and the analysis of participation. These questions will be explored in the *Parmenides*, and the status of immanent characters shifts as the discussion proceeds. For an interpretation of the notion of immanence in Plato, see Fine 1986.

saying "Simmias is large and small"? Isn't that statement still as paradoxical as "the same object is round and square"? Perhaps Socrates' solution is analogous to that in the *Republic*.[20] If we regard immanent characters as parts of the object to which they belong, we can say that Simmias is large and small, because strictly Simmias' largeness is large and his smallness is small, and neither character admits its opposite (102d–103a). The contradiction disappears because different components of Simmias are the proper subjects of those opposites. If this suggestion is correct, immanent characters in the *Phaedo* are assigned the role that physical parts play in the examples in the *Republic*.

We should find this a peculiar way to resolve contradictions, motivated as it is by a feeling of paradox we do not share. And we should not forget our reservations, because the second part of the *Parmenides* will show that the solution generates more puzzles than it solves. For the moment, however, let us ignore our sense of uneasiness and accompany Socrates in his proposal that forms dissolve the paradox. We now turn to his long speech.

Socrates asks Zeno whether he acknowledges that "there is a form, itself by itself, of likeness, and another form, opposite to this, which is what unlike is" (129a). According to Socrates, we need not be astonished that you and I are both like and unlike. Both opposites can be ascribed to us because we get a share of the forms of likeness and unlikeness, and come to be like and unlike to just the extent that we get a share. Similarly, if someone were to demonstrate that Socrates is both one and many, there would be nothing astonishing about that either (129c–d). He could show that Socrates is many by pointing out that his right side is different from his left, his front from his back, and likewise with his upper and lower parts. He thus shows that Socrates partakes of multitude. To show that Socrates is one, he need only point out that Socrates is one person among the seven people present. Socrates is one, because he also partakes of oneness. What would be astonishing, says Socrates (129d–130a), is if someone, having distinguished forms as separate from their participants, could show that the forms themselves partake of opposites—that likeness itself is unlike, unlikeness like, the one

---

20. Cf. Jordan 1983, 42–43; McCabe 1994, 50.

itself many, and the many one. Socrates' challenge to Parmenides and Zeno is to show that the difficulty Zeno displayed in the case of visible things is also displayed in the case of forms. Much in Socrates' speech is underdetermined, and Parmenides opens his interrogation by asking for clarification:

> "Tell me. Have you yourself distinguished as separate, in the way you mention, certain forms themselves, and also as separate the things that partake of them? And do you think that likeness itself is something, separate from the likeness we have? And one and many and all the things you heard Zeno read about a while ago?" "I do indeed," Socrates replied. (130b)

Here Parmenides gets Socrates to confirm two points that were not explicit in his presentation. First, separation is a symmetrical relation. Socrates said in his speech that forms are distinguished as separate from the things that partake of them (129d). He now agrees that things that partake of forms are also separate from them. Second, Socrates agrees that likeness itself is separate from the likeness we have. In discussing the *Phaedo* I used the label "immanent characters" to designate features of objects that forms are invoked to explain. I also suggested that the *Phaedo* dissolves the apparent contradiction in the statement "Simmias is large and small" by treating immanent characters as parts of the object to which they belong. On that view Simmias is large because, strictly speaking, his largeness is large, and he is small because, strictly speaking, his smallness is small. In his speech in the *Parmenides* Socrates speaks of properties that forms explain, but the status of these entities is far from plain.[21] Does he regard

---

21. For instance, in his speech Socrates mentioned entities he called "the likes themselves" and "the unlikes," and he claimed that it would be a marvel if anyone showed that the likes come to be unlike or the unlikes like (129b). Is he talking about immanent characters (the likes in you and me) and claiming (as in the *Phaedo*) that they cannot be characterized by their opposite? Or does he use the plural to specify a single form? Does he identify the immanent character with the form? On the curious phrase "the likes themselves," cf. *Phaedo* 74c, where Socrates speaks of "the equals themselves." For alternative interpretations of these odd locutions, see Ross 1953, 25; Geach 1956, 269; Owen 1968, 230–31; and Wedin 1977.

them as parts of the objects to which they belong? Whatever he thinks about the status of immanent characters, his answer to Parmenides' question confirms that he believes that forms are separate from them. As we shall see, Socrates' agreement on this point will be a source of trouble for his theory.[22]

Parmenides does not ask, and so we do not yet know, precisely what Socrates understands by "separation." The expression could indicate merely that forms are distinct from their participants and immanent characters and vice versa (as we might say that any two non-identical entities are distinct from each other). Or it might mean something stronger—for instance, that forms exist apart from their participants and the immanent characters and vice versa (as we might say of two objects in space, such as a table and a chair not in contact, that they are spatially separate; or of two events in time, such as the writing of the *Parmenides* and the stabbing of Julius Caesar, that they are temporally separate). Two objects are separate in this way if they have no common parts. Alternatively, separation might be construed as ontological independence. Two items are separate in this sense if the nature of the one does not involve the nature of the other. For example, two chemical elements, say copper and tin, are not only distinct from but also ontologically independent of each other. Bronze, on the other hand, is ontologically dependent on both, since its nature involves the natures of copper and tin.[23] The notion of separation is important in the *Parmenides*, and its meaning is left vague at this stage of the argument. As we shall see, Parmenides will exploit different meanings in different parts of his interrogation.

In his initial request for clarification, Parmenides does not question the crucial point of Socrates' solution: his insistence that forms themselves are not subject to the compresence of opposites. The point is vital for Socrates' position, because forms are supposed to explain such compresence in other things. If

---

22. See below, pp. 37–38.

23. This third notion is unlikely to be what Socrates means by separation in his speech. If it is, he makes a serious mistake agreeing with Parmenides that separation between forms and their participants is symmetrical. Forms can be ontologically independent of their participants, but their participants depend on forms for what they are. My three alternatives

they were themselves subject to the same problem, he would have to seek a further solution to dissolve the problem for them. For Socrates that would mean positing further entities, just as he posited forms at first to solve the original problem. If the entities that are supposed to solve the problem are themselves subject to the same problem, the proposal yields an explanatory regress, not a solution. So Socrates asserts that forms are what they are by themselves and do not admit their opposites. He ends his speech by challenging Zeno and Parmenides to show that this is not so—that the same difficulty that Zeno discussed in the case of visible things infects intelligible objects as well, the objects he calls forms (129d–130a). This is the challenge that Parmenides takes up in Part II. But first he calls attention to a variety of difficulties that infect Socrates' theory.[24]

Parmenides' Criticisms (130b–134e)

Parmenides' examination of Socrates' theory divides into six movements, which I label for convenience: (1) Scope of Forms (130b–e), (2) Whole-Part Dilemma (130e–131e), (3) Largeness Regress (132a–b), (4) Forms Are Thoughts (132b–c), (5) Likeness Regress (132c–133a), and (6) Separation Argument (133a–134e).[25]

---

are not exhaustive. For another alternative, see Fine 1980, 205; she acknowledges that her alternative is not in play here (Fine 1984, 58–59).

24. To appreciate the *Parmenides* as a unified whole, it is essential to take note of Socrates' challenge and to expect a response from Parmenides. Teloh (1976) is right to emphasize the dramatic significance of Socrates' challenge, but wrong to claim that Parmenides' response comes in the first part of the dialogue. Parmenides responds to Socrates' challenge in the second part of the dialogue, and the full implications of that response become clear only when one rethinks the whole discussion in light of its ending. This issue will be discussed in the final section of the introduction.

25. Since the publication of Vlastos 1954, the primary attraction of the *Parmenides* has been the two regress arguments listed above as (3) and (5), which Aristotle later referred to under the blanket title "Third Man" (neither version of Plato's argument concerns man, but Aristotle's version does). Much philosophical talent has been devoted to clarifying the logic of the argument, to characterizing its suppressed premises,

His interrogation focuses on two fundamental questions: First (movement 1), What is the scope of forms—that is, What forms are there? And second (movements 2, 5), What is the nature of the relation between physical objects and forms—the relation known as "participation"? Socrates' inability to explain participation also prompts a third question: On what grounds does he regard each form as one, and are those grounds viable (movements 3, 4)? Parmenides reveals the inadequacy of Socrates' position by repeatedly showing that forms are not one but many.

When Socrates finally recognizes that he lacks an adequate account of participation, Parmenides suggests, in the final movement (6), that perhaps there is no relation between physical objects and forms. Entities in each group are related only to other entities in their own group. But then, if we in our realm have no relation to forms and they in theirs have no relation to us, what import can they have for us? Socrates in his long speech had claimed that physical objects have the properties they have by partaking of forms. It now appears that if forms exist but have no relation to us then they don't explain anything. Nor do they ground our knowledge, since we have no access to them. So the question we are left with at the end of Parmenides' interrogation is: Why posit forms at all?

An introduction is not the place for a detailed commentary on Parmenides' objections and Socrates' alternative proposals, especially since the interpretation of these arguments is highly controversial. Even so, some analysis is needed to show how the arguments are motivated and interrelated, and to indicate difficulties that recur on a larger scale in the second part of the dialogue. The six movements display a progression, and only by recognizing it will we, as modern readers, appreciate the force of the final movement (6), which on its own might strike us as a rather feeble objection, but is presented by Parmenides

---

and to determining whether it is a legitimate objection to the treatment of forms in the *Phaedo* and *Republic*. This introduction is not the place to review that literature. Among the important articles on the subject are: Vlastos 1954, Sellars 1955, Geach 1956, Strang 1963, Vlastos 1969, and Cohen 1971. Aristotle's criticisms of the argument and response to it are discussed by Owen 1965, Code 1982, and Fine 1993.

as the greatest difficulty of all.[26] Indeed, that final argument raises the fundamental questions that drive the second part of the dialogue. This introduction will therefore emphasize points of contact between the arguments and questions that reverberate in Part II.

1. Scope of Forms (130b–e)

Parmenides' questioning in this first movement proceeds in four stages, and the guiding question is: What forms are there? The deeper, unexpressed question is: What grounds are there for positing forms in some cases but not in others? Socrates is quite sure that there are forms of the sorts Parmenides lists at stages one and two, he begins to have doubts about the forms mentioned at stage three, and seems quite sure there aren't forms of the sorts mentioned at stage four, though he is troubled by the possibility that the reasons for positing forms in the other cases might apply here as well.

In his long speech Socrates mentioned very few forms explicitly. He gave a list at 129d–e: "likeness and unlikeness, multitude and oneness, rest and motion, and everything of that sort." When Parmenides opens his interrogation by asking for clarification (130b, quoted above), he first poses a question about forms generally and then focuses on one form: Does Socrates think that likeness itself is something, separate from the likeness we have? He then extends the question to one and many and all the things Socrates heard Zeno read about in his book. Included at stage one, apparently, are forms for all the opposites mentioned in Zeno's arguments. Plato has not given us a complete list, and we are left to wonder how extensive the list should be.[27] By chance we have one fragment from Zeno's book that

---

26. Some scholars think (on the basis of 133b4) that the final argument is presented merely as the greatest difficulty among those remaining (further difficulties that Parmenides alludes to at 133b and 135a but does not present). But at 133a he asks, apparently in reference to the preceding five arguments, whether Socrates sees how great the difficulty is for one who posits forms. At 133a–b he then says that Socrates does not yet have an inkling of how great the difficulty is. It is this claim that suggests that Parmenides regards the final argument as a greater difficulty than the previous five.

27. Cf. *Phaedrus* 261d, which lists in connection with Zeno the same

is certainly genuine,[28] and it treats the opposites limited and unlimited. Would Socrates include the members of this pair as forms at stage one? We should recall this passage when we turn to the second part of the dialogue. Parmenides will give a series of deductions hypothesizing first that one is, and then that one is not. In the course of these deductions he will argue that the one is characterized by both, or neither, of a series of opposites. The opposites include one and many, like and unlike, in motion and at rest, which Socrates listed as forms in his speech. The deductions also include being and not-being, limited and unlimited, same and different, equal and unequal, largeness and smallness, in contact and not in contact, and various other pairs. In reading the *Parmenides*, we should ask ourselves whether Socrates would (or should) include all of these opposed pairs as forms at stage one.

Parmenides next asks (stage two, 130b) whether Socrates thinks there are forms of just, beautiful, and good, and everything of that sort. Moral and aesthetic concepts were the focus of Socrates' interest in the early dialogues, and they are regularly cited as forms in the *Phaedo* and the *Republic*.[29]

At stage three (130c) Parmenides asks whether there is a form of human being, separate from us all, and forms of fire and water. At this point Socrates begins to hesitate. If we recall Socrates' speech, the reason for his hesitation may not be far

---

three pairs of opposites that Socrates mentions in his speech: Zeno is said to be able to make the same things appear to his audience as like and unlike, one and many, and at rest and in motion.

28. Quoted in n.16 above.

29. Notice that the good is here listed as one form among others; apparently the preeminent status it enjoys in *Republic* VI and VII is ignored. The good does not figure prominently in the *Parmenides*, but it does in the *Timaeus* and the *Philebus*, and at least the second of these works postdates the *Parmenides*. The ancient testimony about Plato's obscure Lecture on the Good might indicate that Plato identified the good and the one (Aristoxenus, *Elementa Harmonica* 2.30,16–31,3). Aristoxenus' claim is ambiguous, however, and may simply indicate that Plato thought that the good is one—i.e., that there is just one good. But if Plato identified the good and the one, perhaps the good is lurking in the background in the upcoming discussion of oneness in Part II.

to seek. He introduced forms to explain the compresence of opposites. He posited forms of likeness and unlikeness to explain how the same thing can be both like and unlike. The predicate "human being" does not occasion the same uneasiness as do "beautiful," "large," and "like." When Simmias is observed from different perspectives or in different comparisons, perception gives us different reports about his looks and size. He appears beautiful to your eyes but not to mine, large in relation to Socrates but small in relation to Phaedo, like Phaedo in looks but not in size. There is no comparable problem in the case of his being a human being, because perception does not report the opposite.

In *Republic* VII (523a–524e) Socrates says that some of our sense perceptions do, whereas others do not, provoke our thought to reflection. Perceptions that prompt our reflection are those that yield an opposite perception at the same time. He holds up three fingers, the little finger, ring finger, and middle finger, and points out that each of them appears to be a finger. Since sight gives no opposite impression, ordinary people aren't stimulated to ask: What is a finger? Perception of a finger does not compel them to call upon their intellect. The situation is different with largeness and smallness, hardness and softness, and other perceptual features, because sight reports, for example, that the ring finger is large in relation to the little finger but small in relation to the middle finger. Here the visual report seems inadequate, telling us as it does that the same thing is both large and small. So we are provoked to call upon our intellect and to ask: What is largeness? What is smallness?

This passage does not say that there is a form of largeness and not a form of finger, but it corroborates the impression, given by his long speech in the *Parmenides*, that Socrates posits forms to explain the compresence of opposites. In the case of physical objects like human beings, and stuffs like fire and water, perception does not raise an immediate problem about what they are. He therefore feels no comparable need to posit a form. Socrates is represented in the *Parmenides* as young and inexperienced. At the end of the first movement of the cross-examination (130e) and again in the transition to Part II (135c–d), Parmenides attributes Socrates' difficulties to his youth and lack of training. As a novice he is provoked to reflection by the obviously difficult cases, like largeness and smallness, without fully appreciating that perception on its own may also be inadequate in cases that involve no obvious perceptual conflict, like human being, fire, and water.

At stage three, we as readers are invited to ask why forms are posited in some cases but not in others. What are the reasons for positing forms of physical objects and stuffs?[30] Does Zeno's problem—the compresence of opposites—infect these cases too? Is Zeno's problem just one reason among others for positing forms? Is it even perhaps the wrong reason for positing them? Maybe Socrates should go back to stages one and two and reconsider his justification for positing forms in those cases.

The mandate to consider when and why forms are needed is repeated with greater force at stage four, where Socrates balks at the proposal that there may be forms of things that seem undignified and worthless, like hair, mud, and dirt (130c–d). At 130e Parmenides says that Socrates' reluctance is a sign of his inexperience. Is he suggesting that there is a form whenever we call a number of things by the same name—and is he saying that Socrates will eventually recognize that fact?[31] Or is he merely calling to Socrates' attention that he needs a better reason for denying that there are forms of hair, mud, and dirt than that they seem base and worthless? What problem or problems are forms supposed to solve? Does a Platonist need a form of mud,

---

30. *Philebus* 15a mentions a form of human being, and *Timaeus* 51b mentions a form of fire. It is debatable whether the form of fire or merely the physical stuff is being discussed at *Phaedo* 103c–105c. This topic is discussed by Nehamas 1973, 482–90, and Gallop 1975, 197–99.

31. On this question, cf. also 135b–c. A sentence in *Republic* X (596a) has often been taken to make this claim, but long ago J. A. Smith argued that the usual translation of it is grammatically unjustified. On Smith's revised translation the sentence merely claims that if there is a form that form is one (Smith 1917, 71). On this topic see also Fine 1980, 212–20; cf. Moravcsik 1963, 54. In the *Statesman* the Eleatic Visitor, in discussing the method of division, says that divisions should be made at the proper joints (262a–263a; cf. *Phaedrus* 265e–266b). For instance, it is a mistake to divide the class of human beings into Greek and barbarian. The latter is not a proper group because it includes all persons who are non-Greek. Although there is a common name "barbarian," this passage suggests that it would be inappropriate to posit a corresponding form.

for instance, if there are forms of earth and water?[32] If forms perform an explanatory role, perhaps mixtures of stuffs could be explained by reference to the forms of stuffs that compose the mixture. And what about the functional parts of a thing, for instance, a human finger or human hair? Does the Platonist need a form of finger or hair, if there is a form of human being? Could one perhaps explain what a finger or hair is, if one understood what a human being is?[33]

These concrete questions take us beyond the *Parmenides*, but they point toward a more abstract question that guides much of the discussion in the second part of the dialogue: If an entity is composed of parts (as mud is composed of earth and water, and a human being of various functional and non-functional parts), what is the relation between the whole and its parts? Is the whole the same as the aggregate of the parts? If so, perhaps there must be forms corresponding to each of the parts, so that an account of the whole can be given by enumerating the parts. Or is the whole different from all the parts? If so, what relevance do the parts have to an account of the whole? In that case perhaps we need only a form of the whole. Or is the relation between whole and parts of some special sort? If so, that too would affect our decision about what forms there are.[34]

2. Whole-Part Dilemma (130e–131e)

Parmenides now turns to the question: What is the relation between physical objects and forms? Socrates' own proposals in this and the arguments that follow, as well as Parmenides' suggestions on Socrates' behalf, also bear on another question: What sort of entities are forms?

Parmenides starts, as he did at the beginning of the first

---

32. The Greek word translated in the *Parmenides* as "mud" is used in the *Theaetetus* more specifically for clay. In the *Theaetetus* Socrates offers a definition of clay as "earth mixed with liquid" (147c).

33. On the function of hair it is worth consulting *Timaeus* 76c–d, where Timaeus tells us that our creator gave us hair on our heads to protect our brains.

34. On parts and wholes in Part II, see below, pp. 77–79, 87–91. The topic is discussed by Harte 1994. Cf. also *Theaetetus* 203c–205e, and Burnyeat 1990, 191–209.

movement, by clarifying what he takes to be Socrates' position and asking for confirmation:

> "But tell me this: is it your view that, as you say, there are certain forms, from which these other things, by getting a share of them, derive their names – as, for instance, they come to be like by getting a share of likeness, large by getting a share of largeness, and just and beautiful by getting a share of justice and beauty?"
>
> "It certainly is," Socrates replied. (130e–131a)

Socrates said nothing expressly about names in his speech, but Parmenides' proposal spells out Socrates' claim that things that get a share of likeness come to be like. If some sticks and stones come to be like by getting a share of likeness, then by having a share of likeness they can be called by the name "like," derived from the name of the form.

Parmenides' opening statement, with its reference to names, is highly reminiscent of the opening move in the final argument for the immortality of the soul in the *Phaedo*, suggesting that our present argument could helpfully be read in the light of that discussion.[35] In the *Phaedo* Socrates gives what he calls a "safe" explanation of why beautiful things are beautiful. He claims that their beauty is not explained by their bright color or shape or anything like that. The one thing he is sure of is that the form of the beautiful makes them beautiful. He admits that he is unclear about precisely how the form makes them beautiful— that is, he is vague about what the relation is between the form and the things whose character it explains. He says:

> "Nothing else makes it beautiful except the presence or communion, or whatever the manner of its occurrence, of that beautiful. I stop short of affirming that, but affirm only that it is by the beautiful that all the beautiful things are beautiful." (100d)

To understand how the beautiful makes things beautiful, we need to understand the relation between the form and the things whose character it explains. The converse relation, between physical objects and a form, is known as "participation." In our

---

35. For Plato's views on eponymy (naming things after forms in which they participate), see the debate between F. C. White 1977 and Bestor 1978, 1980.

dialogue Parmenides presses Socrates for an account of partici-pation.[36]

Parmenides proposes two alternatives, and Socrates agrees that they are exhaustive.[37] Does each thing that gets a share of a form get as its share the whole form or only a part of it?[38] Let us reformulate the question in terms of immanent characters: When something partakes of a form, does it get as its immanent character the whole of the form or only a part of it? For instance, when Simmias partakes of the form of largeness, is the largeness in him the whole of largeness or merely a part of it?

Consider the first side of the dilemma: Can a whole form— one thing—be in each of a number of things? If so, won't the form be separate from itself by being, as a whole, in things that are separate from each other (131a–b)?

Socrates advances just three positive proposals during Par-menides' cross-examination in Part I, and each is thought-pro-voking. He now suggests that a form could simultaneously be, as a whole, in each of a number of things, if it is like one and the same day (131b). One and the same day, he says, is in many places at the same time without being separate from itself. If a form is like that, it could be one and the same in all.

Just what is this proposal? What does Socrates mean by "day"? Does he mean one and the same day*time*—some definite period between sunrise and sunset, which is simultaneously present in

36. Two Greek verbs are used in Part I for the notion of participation, *metalambanein*, a process verb, which is rendered as "to get a share," and *metexein*, a state verb, which is rendered as "to partake." Part II adds a third, impersonal verb (with the subject specified in the dative case), *metesti*, also a state verb, which is rendered as "has a share." In Part II Parmenides also occasionally uses the noun *koinonia* (or the corresponding verb), which is rendered as "communion."

37. Later (movement 5) Socrates will propose another alternative (132c–d). With the present passage cf. *Philebus* 15b, which mentions the same alternatives and appears to endorse the same conclusion.

38. Recall that earlier I suggested that Socrates treats largeness in Sim-mias as a part of Simmias. Now Parmenides wants to know whether the share Simmias gets is a part of the form. For an interpretation of the *Phaedo* that finds there the model of participation criticized here, see Denyer 1983. The background for the model in Anaxagoras is dis-cussed by Furley 1992, esp. 78–80.

Athens and Thebes? Or one and the same day*light*—an invisible, homogeneous stuff that covers many different places at the same time? Perhaps Plato is prodding us, as readers, to consider the implications of these alternatives. One question we might ask is why Socrates proposes an analogy at all. If he had been born a century later and had attended Aristotle's lectures in the Lyceum, he might have retorted: "Parmenides, if you think a form is separate from itself, by being simultaneously in a number of things, you misunderstand the nature of forms. Forms are universals, and the nature of a universal just is to be present in many places at the same time and to be predicated in common of a number of things.[39] Universals are not thereby separated from themselves." But Aristotle's distinction between universals and particulars had not yet been formulated, and Socrates may not appreciate the distinction. On one interpretation of his analogy, he seems to conceive of forms as abstract objects, on the other as homogeneous invisible stuffs.

Readers sometimes fault Parmenides for not taking Socrates' proposal seriously and for intimidating him into accepting his own less auspicious analogy instead.[40] Perhaps Parmenides recognizes that Socrates' analogy can be interpreted in more than one way and proposes his own to see if that is what Socrates had in mind. In any case, Parmenides switches the analogy from the day to a sail (131b), and Socrates hesitantly accepts the replacement. If we cover a lot of people with a sail, we might say that one thing is over many. This analogy, though less provocative than Socrates' own, has the one advantage of removing the previous ambiguity. Like one and the same daylight, which is simultaneously in many places, or like a sail that covers a lot of people, one and the same form is in many participants.

Parmenides' analogy leads into the second side of the dilemma. If a form is like a sail, isn't a part of it over each person? When Socrates concedes that different parts of the sail are over different people, Parmenides points out that in that case forms are divisible, and things that partake of them partake of a part.

---

39. Aristotle defines a universal in these ways at *De Interpretatione* 7, 17a39–40, and *Metaphysics* Z.16, 1040b25–26.

40. One interpretation that makes much of this change of analogies is Crombie 1963, 325–53. On the analogies, see Panagiotou 1987.

Contrary to what Socrates intended with his own analogy, only part of the form is in each thing. In that case forms are not merely divisible but actually divided into parts. If a form is divided into parts, will it still be one?[41]

The whole-part dilemma treats forms as though they were quantities of stuff that things get a share of. The question is whether a participant gets the whole of the stuff as its share or whether it gets a part of it. If Simmias gets a share of largeness, is the largeness he gets—the character immanent in him—largeness as a whole or a part of largeness? Think of a proper stuff like gold. If we conceive of gold as the element with atomic number 79, we could say that gold, as a whole, is in each of the golden things, because the nature of gold is wholly present in each instance. So gold is separate from itself by being, as a whole, in things that are separate from each other (first side of the dilemma). If, on the other hand, we conceive of gold, as a whole, as the totality of gold, it is the sum of all the instances of gold in the world, whether in coins or jewelry, dust or nuggets, or still in the ground. Gold, as a whole, is split up into bits and scattered around in the various golden things (second side of the dilemma). We can accept both alternatives in the case of material stuffs, because we mean different things by "whole" in the two situations, and both seem to make good sense. But Socrates finds both sides of the dilemma disturbing. How can forms, each of which he takes to be one, be separate from themselves or be aggregates of scattered parts?

In the next section (131c–e) Parmenides makes great fun of the view that forms are analogous to quantities of stuff by focusing on forms of quantities. He states a series of paradoxes that turn on two conceptions of forms and immanent characters that come

---

41. Note that once Socrates concedes that each person is under part of the sail and hence that the sail is divisible, he has already conceded that his one form is many, without Parmenides' further argument that the form is actually divided. For recall that in his long speech he argued that he himself is many, because his right side is different from his left, his front different from his back, and so on. He is many even though he is not actually divided into parts. Given that argument, he must admit that a form is many if it is divisible, whether or not it is actually divided. I owe this observation to Verity Harte.

into blatant conflict in these cases. First, Parmenides and Socrates appear to agree that forms and immanent characters have the same property—the property whose presence in things the form is invoked to explain—just as the stuff gold and portions of gold are both golden. So both largeness itself and largeness in Simmias are large. Second, on the conception of forms and immanent characters as wholes and parts, the whole is larger than each of its parts, and each part is smaller than the whole. Given these two conceptions, there are paradoxes in the case of largeness, equality, and smallness.

Notice that the paradoxical result in the case of the small turns on the assumption that the form of smallness is small: the small is small, because that is its proper character, but also large, because it is a whole, which is larger than each of its parts. Parmenides also says, in discussing largeness, that "things are large by a part of largeness smaller than largeness itself" (131d), which clearly implies that largeness is large. Largeness is large for two reasons—both in the way that smallness is small, because that is its proper character, and in the way that smallness is large, because it is a whole, which is larger than each of its parts. The assumption that smallness is small, that largeness is large, and generally that F-ness is F is known as the "Self-Predication Assumption."[42] This assumption will figure in the two regress arguments to follow.

At the end of the whole-part dilemma, Parmenides asks: "Socrates, in what way, then, will things get a share of your forms, if they can do so neither by getting parts nor by getting wholes?" (131e). Socrates admits that he is stumped. In the next argument, Parmenides shifts the focus from the problem of participation, with its unwelcome result that each form is many, to Socrates' ground for thinking that a form is one. And once he establishes Socrates' ground, he will use that ground to show, to Socrates' dismay once again, that the form is after all many.

3. Largeness Regress (132a–b)

This time Parmenides does not start his argument by asking for clarification. In proposing a reason why Socrates might think

---

42. Interpretations of this assumption are discussed in detail by Malcolm 1991.

each form is one, he goes beyond anything Socrates has said in his speech. Since we will discuss the whole argument and return to it in later sections, I number Parmenides' paragraphs for reference:

> (1) "I suppose you think each form is one on the following ground: whenever some number of things seem to you to be large, perhaps there seems to be some one character, the same as you look at them all, and from that you conclude that the large is one."
> "That's true," he said. (132a)

What is the proposal? Is Parmenides saying that whenever Socrates looks at a number of things—temples and elephants, say—all of which seem to him to be large, he notices that they share one common character, largeness, and from that concludes that the large is one? Is Parmenides suggesting that Socrates takes the character he observes in the various large things to be the form? If so, then he takes Socrates to identify the form with the immanent character. At the same time, Parmenides' claim that Socrates observes some *one* character exhibited in *many* large things might indicate that he takes Socrates to regard the form as what Aristotle would later call a "universal"—one thing that is present in many places at the same time, or naturally predicated of a number of things.[43]

This interpretation has one serious drawback. The passage suggests that Socrates makes an inference. He is supposed to conclude that the large is one on the basis of what he notices about the many large things. What he noticed was some one character. If the one character he notices just is the form, what inference has he made when he concludes that the character is one?

Perhaps Parmenides is making a different point, and perhaps our translation has caused us to miss the inference that Socrates is supposed to make. Let us try the following translation (with changes from the previous version italicized):

> (1*) "I suppose you think *there is one form in each case* on the following ground: whenever some number of things seem to you to be large, perhaps there seems to be some one character, the same as you look

---

43. See citations in n.39 above.

at them all, and from that you conclude that *there is one the large* (*hen to mega . . . einai*)."

"That's true," he said. (132a)

According to this translation, the passage concerns the *existence* of one the large and not merely the *oneness* of the large. This proposal has an advantage over the previous one in that it allows Socrates to make a genuine inference. He observes a group of things that all seem to share one character, largeness, and on the basis of that observation he concludes that there exists one form, the large. On this interpretation Socrates sees the immanent character and makes an inference about the form.[44] The character he sees is distinct from the form he posits.

In *Republic* V Socrates talks about some people he calls the lovers of sights and sounds (475d–480a). These people accept the existence of many beautifuls.[45] What they refuse to accept is phrased in Greek just as in our passage: *hen to kalon . . . einai* ("there is one the beautiful" or "the beautiful is one") (479a). Perhaps in our passage Parmenides is saying that Socrates differs from the lovers of sights: Whereas they refuse to infer, on the basis of the existence of many beautifuls, that there exists one the beautiful, Socrates makes the inference.

A disadvantage of this proposal is that it ignores the context of the Largeness Regress, following the Whole-Part Dilemma and preceding the argument Forms Are Thoughts. In the Whole-Part Dilemma Parmenides and Socrates both assumed that the form is one, and Parmenides asked how one form could be in many things (131a). He argued that if the form is in many things, then it is not one but divided into many (131c). This conclusion prompts him now to ask: Why does Socrates assume that a form is one? Are his grounds for that assumption adequate? Parmenides will show that Socrates' grounds are inadequate by arguing once again that his form is many, this time by reduplication. In the next argument (Forms Are Thoughts) Socrates offers

---

44. See the note on "character" at 132a of the translation. Cf. Cornford 1939, 88 and note. For another instance of Plato's use of *idea* for the immanent character as distinct from the form, see *Timaeus* 28a.

45. Scholars disagree about whether these people accept the existence of many beautiful things or many kinds of beauty. Another possibility is that they think beauty in things is (numerically) many.

a new proposal to guard the oneness of his forms from Parmenides' objections: If a form is a thought that occurs in many minds, can't it be one and escape the previous difficulties (132b)? In these arguments the existence of the form the large is not in question, but its oneness is. The movements in Part I display a marked progression, and the Largeness Regress is a step in that progression. Its placement in the series is a good reason to keep the original translation (1) and to try to find a plausible interpretation of it.

What else might Parmenides be proposing? He could be making the following suggestion: Whenever Socrates looks at a number of things that all seem to him to be large, he thinks that some one character is the same in all the cases, and from that he concludes that the form corresponding to that character is one. As on the previous interpretation, Socrates sees the immanent character and makes an inference about the form. On the basis of seeing one immanent character (let's call it "the large in us") that occurs in many things, he infers that the form which corresponds to that character is one.

In the argument that follows, Parmenides reveals the inadequacy of Socrates' grounds for that conclusion. He continues:

> (2) "What about the large itself and the other large things? If you look at them all in the same way with the mind's eye, again won't some one thing appear large, by which all these appear large?"[46]
> "It seems so." (132a)

---

46. The standard translation of paragraph (2) (with alteration italicized) is:

> (2*) "What about the large itself and the other large things? If you look at them all in the same way with the mind's eye, *won't some one large again appear*, by which all these appear large?"

The use of *phaneitai* ("will appear") as a complete predicate in (2*) would fit nicely with the second translation of the first paragraph (1*) that we discussed above. Just as (1*) gave Socrates a ground for supposing the existence of one form the large, so (2*) would force him to concede the existence of a second form the large. On this view paragraph (3) opens with Parmenides repeating what Socrates has just conceded in response to paragraph (2*). It then goes on to point out that he must now admit a third form, and so on.

I prefer (2) to (2*) on both syntactic and philosophical grounds, but

(3) "So another form of largeness will make its appearance, which has emerged alongside largeness itself and the things that partake of it, and in turn another over all these, by which all of them will be large. Each of your forms will no longer be one, but unlimited in multitude." (132a–b)

In paragraph (2) things start to get peculiar. Socrates is asked to repeat the performance described in paragraph (1), but this time with his mind's eye: just as he looked at the many large things at the outset, he is to look in the same way (but with his mind's eye) at the large itself, together with the other large things. Why does Parmenides propose this as a possible performance, and why does Socrates allow him to derive the consequences he does? If on the first round Socrates took the form simply to be the common character (as in the first interpretation of paragraph [1] we considered), why does he now agree to look at it together with its instances? A common character is what we now call a universal. Is the common character that temples and elephants share itself large? Except for certain unusual universals, like oneness and being, most universals are not instances of themselves.

I confine myself here to the syntax (the philosophical point can wait until we discuss the Separation Argument below). The last two clauses of paragraph (2) are parallel in the Greek, as in the translation. Although the verb *phainetai* ("appears") can be used absolutely (i.e., as a complete predicate) as in (2*), and is so used once (by my counting) in the *Parmenides* (at 165b1), it is typically used as an incomplete predicate: for ordinary usage, see, e.g., 131d2 and 132c8; for repeated use, see Deduction 7 (164b–165e). The verb *anaphainetai* ("makes its appearance") is available for absolute use and occurs in paragraph (3) (132a10; cf. Likeness Regress, 132e7). (Vlastos 1969, 299 n.32, who wants an absolute construction in both paragraphs, erroneously claims that the same verb is used on both occasions.)

For the philosophical consideration, see below, p. 49. At present I simply suggest that one consider two possibilities for the function of "So" (*ara*) at the beginning of paragraph (3). Is Parmenides saying "So (we agree that)," and does the first sentence of (3) open by repeating what Socrates has already conceded in response to paragraph (2) or (2*)? Or does "So" mark a new inference based on what Socrates has conceded in response to (2)? If the latter, what has Parmenides said in (2) on the basis of which he concludes in (3) that there is a second and then a third form of largeness?

We saw in the previous argument that Parmenides derived paradoxes in the case of the large, the equal, and the small by relying on two conceptions of forms and immanent characters that come into conflict in the case of forms of quantities. One of those was a self-predication assumption: both F-ness itself and F-ness in us are F—for example, both largeness itself and largeness in Simmias are large. That discussion, however, treated forms not as universals but as analogous to material stuffs. It is not odd to think that the stuff gold is golden, but it is quite odd to think that the universal gold is golden, that the universal justice is just, or that the universal largeness is large.[47]

If forms are universals but self-predicating, perhaps the relation between subject and character differs from that in ordinary predications. For instance, perhaps "justice is just" is not a predication but an identity-statement (in which the predicate reidentifies the subject). Or perhaps it is shorthand for "justice is whatever it is to be just," where what follows the first "is" (of identity) could be replaced by a definition once we have it.[48] But if we are to understand the "is" in "the large is large" as the "is" of identity, Socrates has no reason to group the form together with the large things. For in that case the large shares no feature in common with them.

Socrates does agree to the grouping, however. Perhaps the form of largeness is regarded in this passage as a cause.[49] If forms are causes, they are not causes in our modern sense: A form is not an event, nor does a form cause an effect by doing something to bring it about. Nonetheless a form is somehow responsible for the effect, and appeal to the form is thought to explain it. As the item responsible, a form can be regarded as a cause.[50]

---

47. Self-predication claims occur occasionally in the dialogues. See *Protagoras* 130c–e and *Hippias Major* 292e. Below we will discuss such a claim at *Phaedo* 100c.

48. For this interpretation of self-predication in the middle dialogues, see Nehamas 1979.

49. The thesis that forms are causes is discussed by Moline 1981, 88–95, and is explored in detail throughout the dialogues by Teloh 1981. On forms as causes in this argument, see also Scaltsas 1992.

50. Aristotle evidently thought that Plato regarded forms as causes: see

Notice that in paragraph (2) Parmenides mentions some one thing *by which* the large itself and the other large things appear large, and in paragraph (3) he speaks of a largeness *by which* the collection, largeness$_1$, largeness$_2$, and the other large things, are large. This causal language should remind us of the "safe" explanation Socrates offered in a passage I quoted earlier from the *Phaedo*: "[I] affirm only that it is *by the beautiful* that all the beautiful things are beautiful" (100d).

Plato probably attributes to Socrates a view about causes that Aristotle would later espouse:[51] A cause has the character that an effect has in virtue of it. Both Plato and Aristotle probably inherited the idea from their predecessors.[52] Consider this passage from the *Phaedo*:

"It appears to me that if anything else is beautiful *besides the beautiful itself*, it is beautiful for no other reason than because it partakes of that beautiful; and the same goes for all cases. Do you assent to that sort of explanation?" (100c)

Here Socrates appears to be claiming that the beautiful itself is beautiful, and that other things are beautiful because they partake of it. The form of the beautiful, which is itself beautiful, explains the beauty of other things.

If Socrates thinks of forms as causes that have the character

---

his criticisms in *Generation and Corruption* II.9, 335b7–20; cf. *Metaphysics* A.9, 991b1–9, and M.5.

51. Aristotle, *Physics* III.2, 202a9–12; VIII.5, 257b9–10; cf. *Metaphysics* a.1, 993b23–26.

52. Perhaps the most vivid statement is Anaxagoras DK 59 B10: "How could hair come to be from not hair and flesh from not flesh?" Cf. Alcmaeon (DK 24 B4), translated in Freeman 1948, and the ancient medical treatises *On the Nature of Man* 7 and *On Tradition in Medicine* 13–16 (Lloyd 1978). For further evidence, see Moline 1981, esp. 84–88. In the Presocratics the item responsible for an effect is often a stuff (what Aristotle would later call a material cause). But whether one takes the item responsible to be a stuff (Presocratics), a form (Plato), or an efficient cause (Aristotle), the idea is the same: the item responsible has the character that the result has in virtue of it. This causal thesis enjoyed a long tradition through the Middle Ages and reappears in Descartes, *Meditation* III.

they explain in other things, then he should be prepared to view (with his mind's eye) the large itself together with the other large things, since it shares with them a common character.

But now we must ask why he permits Parmenides to generate a regress. If Socrates believes that a form *explains* the character that other things have, he should insist that the form itself needs no further explanation. Otherwise his theory is indeed subject to the regress Parmenides describes. In his speech Socrates mentioned "a form, itself by itself, of likeness," and he said that other things get a share of it (129a). It is by getting a share of likeness that things come to be like and by having a share that they are like. Does he think that likeness itself is like by having a share of likeness? Notice that Socrates says that a form is "itself by itself." This phrase can be understood in more than one way,[53] and on one construal something is itself by itself, if it is itself responsible for its own proper being, independently of other things. If Socrates thinks that forms are causes, he should think that forms are what they are by—in virtue of, because of— themselves, not by, or because of, something other than themselves. Yet if that is what he thinks, why in our argument does he allow the regress? He should object that other things are large because of largeness but largeness itself is large because of itself.

Socrates does not challenge the regress, however, apparently agreeing that the large itself is large because of something other than itself. Scholars have supposed that he is relying on a tacit Non-Identity Assumption, which they formulate in various ways—e.g., the form that accounts for the class of F things cannot itself be a member of that class,[54] or nothing is F in virtue of itself.[55] Obviously he does need to rely on some such assumption, since he permits the regress. The question is why he would make that assumption, given that it so obviously de-

---

53. See note at 129a of the translation.

54. See Malcolm 1991, 48, 62. For Gregory Vlastos's original formulation, see Vlastos 1954, 237. As Vlastos points out, on his own version the Non-Identity and Self-Predication Assumptions are mutually inconsistent. For that reason scholars have looked for alternative formulations of the Non-Identity Assumption.

55. Peterson 1973, 453 (identified as the principle of non-explanation); Fine 1993, 206.

feats the explanatory theory he was defending in his long speech. Socrates is young and inexperienced, but can we find evidence in the text for his trouble here?

Recall Parmenides' initial request for clarification at the conclusion of Socrates' speech (quoted above):

> "Have you yourself distinguished as separate, in the way you mention, certain forms themselves, and also as separate the things that partake of them? And do you think that likeness itself is something, separate from the likeness we have?" (130b)

In discussing this passage earlier,[56] I pointed out that Parmenides made two points explicit that were not explicit in Socrates' own speech: (1) separation between forms and participants is symmetrical; and (2) forms are separate not only from their participants, but also from the immanent character they explain (e.g., likeness we have). I also mentioned that the word "separate" could mean various things, and that its meaning was not clarified by either speaker.

Separation was repeatedly discussed in the first movement of Parmenides' interrogation, on the scope of forms. While Socrates agreed at stages one, two, and three that the forms mentioned are separate from things, at stage four he balked at the idea that forms of undignified stuffs are separate, saying that hair, mud, and dirt are just what we see (130d). This reaction suggests that, in the case of those forms he accepts, he envisages them as existing apart from the things they explain and not as features we perceive in them.

If separate existence is what Socrates means by separation, then in assenting to Parmenides' second proposal at 130b, that likeness itself is separate from the likeness we have, he has agreed to a premiss that Parmenides can use in the Largeness Regress. Socrates' causal theory of forms commits him to regarding largeness itself as large (because it explains that character in other things). So largeness itself can be added to the group of things that share a common immanent character. An immanent character does not exist apart from the objects whose character it is. But now, since Socrates thinks that the form exists apart from the character it explains, the form cannot explain its *own*

---

56. See above, pp. 16–18.

immanent character. So he must posit a further form to account for the immanent character the first form shares with its participants. As a cause, the second form will then have that same character, and so there must be a third form, separate from the second, that accounts for it. And so the regress proceeds. The forms generated by the regress are qualitatively identical but numerically distinct, because each exists apart from its predecessor.

This unwanted consequence results from Socrates' commitment to two theses: first, the view that forms have the character that others things have in virtue of them; and second, the view that forms are separate—exist apart—from the immanent character they explain. Given these two beliefs, each of Socrates' forms, which he regarded as one, turns out to be not one but unlimited in multitude. This time a form is many, not by division, as in the previous argument, but by reduplication.

4. Forms Are Thoughts (132b–c)

In response to the regress argument, Socrates offers his second positive proposal. He claims that if each form is a thought, which properly occurs only in minds, it could be one and not face the previous difficulties.[57] Like his earlier analogy with the day, Socrates' suggestion seems promising. And whereas the day was merely an analogy to show how one and the same form might simultaneously be in a number of things, the present proposal, which is meant to achieve the same result, concerns the nature and status of forms as such. Each form is a thought, and one and the same thought can occur in more than one mind.

Why does Socrates believe that his new suggestion escapes the earlier difficulties? Apparently he thinks that a single form can be in your mind and mine without falling foul of either side of the whole-part dilemma. A thought is neither separate from itself by being simultaneously in several minds nor split up into parts. This time forms do seem to satisfy Aristotle's definition of a universal: Socrates regards a form as a mental item that can occur in many minds.[58]

---

57. An illuminating discussion of this argument is given in Burnyeat 1982, 20–23.

58. In his second objection to Socrates' proposal, however, Parmenides again treats them as though they were stuffs (132c).

Presumably Socrates also thinks his proposal avoids the unlimited duplication that plagued his forms in the largeness regress. But how? Is he rejecting one or both of the assumptions that led to the trouble in that argument? Consider separation: If forms are thoughts that occur in minds, they do not exist apart from the minds whose thoughts they are. Even so, he probably thinks that thoughts exist apart from the concrete objects of which they are thoughts. The thought largeness, which can occur in your mind and mine, corresponds to the largeness we observe in things, but the thought is in our minds, not in the things.[59] What about self-predication? Socrates' proposal seems not to concern participation.[60] If it doesn't, the form need not be viewed as a cause that shares a common feature with its participants. By proposing that forms are thoughts, Socrates may think that he can avoid an infinite regress by avoiding self-predication. If he denies that the thought largeness is large, the thought cannot be viewed with the mind's eye together with the things it is a thought of, as sharing a common feature with them. So there will be no infinite regress of thoughts.

Parmenides raises two objections to Socrates' proposal. In the first he contends that a thought, far from being a form itself, must have a form outside the mind as its object. I take his second objection to attack a possible response to the first objection.

Consider the first objection. Parmenides gets Socrates' agreement that a thought has an object, and that the object is something that is. In agreeing to this, Socrates probably takes himself to concede nothing. His own proposal was that forms are thoughts, and he probably takes such thoughts to have as their object various things in the world.[61] But Parmenides then takes a further step:

> "Isn't it [the thought] of some one thing, which that thought thinks is over all the instances, being some one character?"

---

59. Parmenides will claim otherwise in his second objection (132c).

60. In his second objection (132c) Parmenides will reintroduce it.

61. See the note to the translation at 132b. The content of Socrates' proposal is ambiguous in the Greek. On one construal he explicitly claims that a thought is of various things. On the translation we give in the main text, this claim is merely implicit.

"Yes."

"Then won't this thing that is thought to be one, being always the same over all the instances, be a form?"

"That, too, appears necessary." (132c)

Parmenides' objection is that some thought, for example, largeness, has as its object, not a number of large things, but one entity, largeness—the form—which is over all the instances. By granting this, Socrates is forced back to his position in the previous argument. If the form of largeness is an entity outside the mind which stands in a causal relation to the various large things, it can be grouped together with them, and the regress follows as before.

Has Socrates given in too easily? Why does he agree that the thought is of one form over the many? Why does he not agree that one thought is of one thing but insist that the single object is the immanent character shared by the many? Recall that at the beginning of the previous argument Parmenides gave Socrates the following ground for thinking that each form is one: "whenever some number of things seem to you to be large, perhaps *there seems to be some one character*, the same as you look at them all, and from that you conclude that the large is one" (132a). As I suggested we understand that claim, Socrates notices some one character in various things and concludes that the form corresponding to the character is one. If that understanding was correct, he might now have said the following: "My claim is that the form is a thought in the mind. I can agree that its object is one thing, as you say, but on my view that one thing is a single character present in all the instances. The object of my thought is an immanent character: I needn't posit yet another entity over that character. Thus I can avoid the regress you generated on the previous round."

But can he? Consider the inference in paragraph (1) of the Largeness Regress. Parmenides claims that because Socrates thinks there is some one character which is the same in the various instances, he concludes that the form corresponding to the character is one. Why is he supposed to make this inference? According to Socrates' long speech, things are large because they get a share of the form of largeness. On his view, things have some largeness (an immanent character) in them *because* they get a share of the form. So if there is an immanent character, there is a form that is its cause. He infers the existence of the cause from the existence of its effect. Accordingly, had Socrates in our present argument countered Parmenides' reintroduction of forms outside the mind by claiming that the single object of thought is the immanent character shared by a number of things, Parmenides could have said: "Then if you agree that there is an immanent character, you must infer once again that there is a form that is its cause. So my objection stands. You must face the regress in the previous argument."

Now suppose that Socrates had objected: "No. From the existence of the immanent character I infer only that there is a single thought that occurs in many minds. I have proposed that this is the form." Parmenides could then have said: "Are you now claiming that the thought in our minds *explains* the character in things? Are you saying that things have the character they have because they partake of a thought? I presume you must believe this, given your view that things have the character they have by getting a share of a form. I'll now show you why that is absurd."

I have supplied a good deal, but I take it that Parmenides' second objection in our text turns on Socrates' agreement to the proposals in this tacit exchange. Parmenides says:

> "Given your claim that other things partake of forms, won't you necessarily think either that each thing is composed of thoughts and all things think, or that, although they are thoughts, they are unthinking?" (132c)

If forms are thoughts and account for an immanent character in things, then it is by partaking of thoughts that things have the characters they have. Take a stone. It is a stone and large and has various other properties. Accordingly, the stone partakes of the thought stone and the thought largeness and so on. So either the stone actively thinks, since it is composed of thoughts, or it doesn't think, despite being composed of thoughts. Both alternatives are absurd.

This objection may seem unfair. After all, thought is a formal or ideal feature of forms on Socrates' proposal, not a proper feature. That is, Socrates treats thought as a feature of a form as a form, not as a feature of a form as the form that it is.[62] Why

---

62. On formal features of forms, cf. above p. 10.

should objects take on the formal features of forms as well as their proper features?[63] Recall that Socrates failed to deal with the whole-part dilemma and that he agreed at the time that the two alternatives there mentioned were exhaustive. No other alternative has yet been offered, so Parmenides is free to use the conception of participation assumed in that argument. On that view forms were like quantities of stuff, and things got a bit of that stuff. Since forms are now supposed to be thoughts, a thing that partakes of a form gets a bit of thought-stuff. And so Socrates faces the dilemma Parmenides presents: either all things think, or things, though composed of thoughts, don't think.

5. Likeness Regress (132c–133a)

Socrates now offers his third and final proposal, which squarely addresses the problem of participation with a new alternative. This proposal stands out in contrast with the previous two,[64] because it is not merely an ad hoc solution to a problem at hand, but a view favored elsewhere in Plato's dialogues, including the *Timaeus*.[65] So we may presume that it is a conception Plato himself took very seriously. Socrates says that what appears to him most likely is that forms are like patterns (*paradeigmata*) set in nature (i.e., outside the mind), and other things resemble them and are likenesses (*homoiomata*). Partaking of forms, he says, is simply being modeled on them.

The current proposal about participation is very different from that envisaged in the whole-part dilemma. On that view, if something partakes of a form, it gets a share of it, as though the form were a quantity of stuff that is parceled out to the various participants. On the present view, a form is comparable to an artist's model, and the participants are comparable to the images the artist makes. Participation in the form F-ness, as Socrates

---

63. This question is discussed by Keyt 1971.

64. i.e., his suggestion that a form is like the day (131b) and his suggestion that a form is a thought (132b).

65. One of the issues in dating the *Timaeus* is its use of the model here criticized. See the debate between Owen 1953, 318–22, and Cherniss 1957, 360–78. Several scholars have argued that the *Timaeus* offers a solution to the puzzle in the *Parmenides*. For alternatives, see Waterlow 1982, Prior 1983, and Patterson 1985, 51–62.

describes it, is being a likeness or copy of F-ness. Notice that *being a likeness of* is an asymmetrical relation. If x is a likeness of F-ness, F-ness is not a likeness of x. A portrait is a likeness of Simmias; Simmias is not a likeness of it. Parmenides makes trouble for Socrates' proposal by arguing that the asymmetrical relation is based on an underlying symmetrical relation—the relation of *being like*. If x is like F-ness, F-ness is like x. If a portrait of Simmias is like Simmias, Simmias is like it.

There are two general ways to construe the argument that follows. On one reading, Parmenides generates a regress in much the same way as he did in the earlier argument about largeness.[66] Take any form, say the form of beauty. According to Socrates' proposal, the many beautiful things are beautiful because they are likenesses of the beautiful itself. Parmenides then points out that, if the many beautiful things are likenesses of beauty, not only are they like beauty, but beauty is like them. Since they are like, beauty and its likenesses have a feature in common on the basis of which they are like, namely their beauty. (This time, instead of assuming self-predication, Parmenides infers it from Socrates' proposal.) But since the form that accounts for that character is separate from it (Separation Assumption), a regress follows as before. Another form of beauty will make its appearance to account for the beauty shared by the first form and the other beautiful things. And so on. There is an unlimited multitude of forms that are qualitatively the same but numerically distinct.

The second way to read the argument is to take it as concerning the form of likeness.[67] Read in this way, the regress may be quite different from the previous one. Socrates gets into trouble by failing to recognize that likeness is a relation between entities, not an item that stands in a further relation to the entities it relates. We start as before with any form, say the form of beauty. Both beauty and its likenesses are like each other, so they have a feature in common, namely (both beauty and) likeness. Recall that Socrates claimed in his speech that things are like by getting

---

66. Variations on this general reading are given by Vlastos 1954, 241–44, Hathaway 1973, Lee 1973, Prior 1979, and Spellman 1983.

67. Variations on this reading are given by Allen 1983, 158–68, and Schofield 1996. I have also profited from reading an unpublished paper by Henry Mendell.

a share of likeness. He therefore believes that if the form of beauty and the many beautiful things are like each other, they are like by partaking of likeness. If the many beautiful things and the beautiful itself all partake of likeness, then on the present proposal they are likenesses of likeness. Now the form of likeness, as pattern, is like things that are like it; so it can be grouped together with them on the basis of their common feature, likeness. What ties together this new group? There is no logical reason why a relation should not relate itself to other things, but once more Socrates' commitment to the Separation Assumption prevents him from recognizing this. He agrees that since the form of likeness is like other things, there must be a further form, likeness$_2$, to relate the members of the new collection. And since this new form shares with its participants a common feature, likeness, there must be a fresh form, likeness$_3$, to relate them, and so on indefinitely.

There are several reasons for preferring this interpretation of the argument to the previous one, but the main one is this:[68] Those who adopt an interpretation of the first sort must delete a word from the Greek text at 132d9–e1 to avoid having Parmenides simply repeat himself in his next statement at 132e3–4. The text reads (with the relevant word bracketed):

> "And isn't there a compelling necessity for that which is like to partake of the same one [form] as what is like it?"
> "There is."
> "But if like things are like by partaking of something, won't that be the form itself?"
> "Undoubtedly." (132d9–e5)

On the second interpretation we can keep the word "form," because Parmenides is not repeating himself. Recall that Socrates started with any form, say the form of beauty, and proposed that the many beautiful things are beautiful because they are likenesses of beauty. Parmenides then pointed out that if the likenesses are like beauty, then beauty is like them. In virtue of what are they like? Are they like in virtue of beauty? Or are they like in virtue of likeness? Parmenides' first statement (132d9–e1) is ambiguous, allowing for both possibilities. But his next

---

68. I owe this consideration to Schofield 1996.

statement (132e3–4) makes clear that if things are *like*, it is by partaking of *that*—namely likeness—that they are like.

There is a further indication as well. Parmenides concludes the argument by saying: "So other things don't get a share of the forms *by likeness* (*homoioteti*); we must seek some other means by which they get a share" (133a). Socrates' proposal made no mention of likeness. He spoke of forms as patterns and participants as *likenesses* (*homoiomata*). The mention of likeness at the end of the argument indicates that Parmenides has construed Socrates' proposal about the participation relation as grounded in the form of likeness.

An advantage of this interpretation is that the present argument does not simply repeat the previous one about largeness but exposes a different problem. That argument derived a regress by focusing on a form things partake of, showing that if something partakes of one, it partakes of an unlimited number. This argument derives a regress by focusing on the relation between an object and the form it partakes of, treating the relation as standing to its relata in an analogous relation. At each step the relation that bundled the previous group must itself be bundled together with them. There must then (given the Separation Assumption) be a further relation that bundles them, and so on indefinitely. So an unlimited number of relations are needed to connect an object and its character. The regress resembles one made famous by F. H. Bradley.[69] As we shall see, both sorts of regress are involved in the second part of the dialogue. We will encounter a Bradley-type regress in the fifth deduction of Part II, where Parmenides will again show that our understanding of participation is inadequate.[70]

6. Separation Argument (133a–134e)

Socrates has failed to give an account of participation that is immune to Parmenides' objections. So in the final movement of his interrogation Parmenides assumes that there simply is no relation between physical objects and forms. This assumption

---

69. Bradley 1897, 18. The similarity with Bradley's regress is also pointed out by Ryle 1939, 107.

70. 161e–162b, discussed below pp. 94–99.

is justified, because the preceding discussion has shown that Socrates cannot explain how participation works. So if someone objected that there is no such relation, and hence that forms are unknowable, he would be unable to show the objector that he is wrong (133b–c).

Parmenides' argument has two parts.[71] In the first part (133a–134c) he argues that forms have no relation to us. Moreover, we have no intellectual access to forms but only to things that belong to us and our world. In the second part (134c–e) he argues that the gods are not our masters and that by means of divine knowledge, though much more precise than ours, they know nothing of us.

Several points in the first part of the argument should be noticed. First, Parmenides and Socrates agree that a form, which is "itself by itself," is not *in* us (133c). This idea is contrary to the view they explored in the Whole-Part Dilemma, but it was presupposed in the Largeness Regress, as we interpreted that argument. If a form is "itself by itself," it exists apart from us.[72] Furthermore, not only do forms exist apart from us, they are also ontologically independent of us, and we and things that belong to us are ontologically independent of them.[73] This more radical view of separation is a direct consequence of Socrates' failure in the preceding arguments to provide an acceptable account of the relation between physical objects and forms. Without such an account we must assume a complete separation between forms and us. If forms are separate in this radical sense, they cannot explain the properties that physical objects have.

Parmenides clarifies this point by focusing on forms of relations,[74] such as the form of mastership. He points out that forms

---

71. Interpretations of the argument very different from my own are given by Cornford 1939, 98–99, Forrester 1974, Lewis 1979, Peterson 1981, and McPherran 1983. One author who emphasizes that the argument presents a serious difficulty is Prior 1985, 75–82.

72. See note to the translation at 129a on the ambiguity of the phrase "itself by itself."

73. See p. 17 above for ontological independence as one meaning of "separation."

74. Although Parmenides focuses on forms of relations (such as mastership) and on forms of relational properties (such as master) in marking

are determined as what they are in relation to one another, and that things that belong to us, such as mastership in us, are determined as what they are, not in relation to the forms to which their names correspond, but in relation to other things that belong to us. Thus human masters are what they are in relation to human slaves, not in relation to master itself (133d–134a). There is, then, a total separation between the realm of forms and our visible realm: the causal link between them has been severed.

A second point to notice: Although there is no association between the two realms, Parmenides continues to speak of participation. In this argument participation is a relation, not between ourselves and forms, but between ourselves and the immanent characters that belong to us.[75] He says that whatever we call the things that belong to us, whether likenesses (cf. the previous argument) or something else, it is by partaking of them—the things that belong to us—that we come to be called by their various names (133d). Whereas earlier Parmenides said that we *partake of* (*metechomen*) forms and *have* (*echomen*) immanent characters (130b), in this final argument the two verbs are used synonymously.[76] We neither have nor partake of forms (134b); we both have and partake of immanent characters. In the second part of the argument, Parmenides also says that in the realm of forms, god partakes of and has knowledge itself (134c). So participation, though denied between physical objects and forms, is permitted within each of the two separate spheres. Accordingly, the things we partake of do not exist apart from us. They are *in* us.[77]

---

off the realm of forms from our realm, by the end of the argument that realm appears to include all forms, including those that we would not think of as relational. See 134b–c, where beauty is mentioned.

75. I shall continue to use the label "immanent characters," though in this final movement forms no longer explain them. Immanent characters and corresponding forms simply have the same name.

76. On Plato's usual use of "partakes of" and "has" and the anomaly here, see Fujisawa 1974.

77. We might now ask: Are immanent characters subject to the whole-part dilemma? In partaking of our (human) mastership, does a man have as his share the whole of it or a part of it?

Although the two realms are independent, they seem very similar. In the realm of forms, master itself is what it is in relation to slave itself. In our realm, a human master is what he is in relation to a human slave. There is also knowledge in both realms: knowledge itself is of truth itself, and each particular knowledge (that is, the branches of ideal knowledge, such as ideal arithmetic, geometry, and carpentry) is related to its proper object—to what that object is (134a). Similarly in our realm, our knowledge is of the truth here, and each particular knowledge (our arithmetic, geometry, carpentry) is of its proper object here (134a–b). So we cannot know the truths in that realm, since we do not partake of knowledge itself, but we can know truths that belong to our own realm.

This argument invites us to ask: What is so bad about the situation here envisaged? If things in our realm are determined as what they are in relation to other things in our realm, and if we can know these truths without appealing to forms, what use are forms? Why bother with them?

The main point of the second part of the argument (134c–e) appears to be that the gods partake of knowledge itself and so know the forms, but lack our knowledge, and so do not know us or things in our realm. Shocked by this outcome, which undermines traditional religious belief, Socrates says at the end of the argument: "If god is to be stripped of knowing, our argument may be getting too bizarre" (134e). The argument is no doubt shocking to Greek piety, but is that why Parmenides announces it as the greatest difficulty (133a–b)? It is a shame about the gods, of course. Still, if things in our realm can be known and explained without reference to forms, and if we are empowered within our realm, how much have we lost if we give up forms and gods? According to this argument, they seem irrelevant to us and our concerns.

Are they? At the beginning of the second part of the argument, Parmenides says:

> "Surely you would say that if in fact there is knowledge – a kind itself – it is much more precise than is knowledge that belongs to us. And the same goes for beauty and all the others." (134c)

This statement suggests that we have indeed lost something of importance if we have no access to forms. Our knowledge is not precise like that of the gods, and beauty in us is fuzzy, not something precise. It may be that we can do without forms, but the cost is a loss of precision. Both our knowledge and its objects are somehow nebulous. What does this nebulousness amount to?

In discussing the Largeness Regress (132a–b), we ignored one point that may be significant in answering this question. I suggested that in paragraph (1) of that argument Socrates makes an inference from a belief about an immanent character to a conclusion about the corresponding form. I now suggest that a similar inference occurs in paragraph (3) on the basis of paragraph (2). Notice that in paragraph (2) Parmenides speaks of something that *appears* large and makes other things *appear* large, whereas in paragraph (3) he speaks of a form of largeness that makes other things *be* large.[78] My suggestion is this. In paragraph (2) Parmenides proposes that when Socrates views the large itself together with the other large things, he again notices (but this time with his mind's eye) a common immanent character which accounts for the common appearance. In paragraph (3) Parmenides announces that Socrates must now infer the existence of a second form of largeness to account for the character the first form shares with its participants.[79] As we saw earlier, he must make the inference because he regards the form as separate from the character it explains. On this interpretation, the immanent character accounts for appearances. But given the causal link between the immanent character and the form, the form is responsible for things actually being as they appear to be.

Remove that causal link, as Parmenides does in the Separation Argument, and we no longer have access to what things really are. Also, without a causal link to forms, the characters we observe lose their definiteness. They are imprecise because they are determined as what they are, not by certain fixed relations to unchanging forms (what we might call a "vertical causality"), but by their changing relations to other things in our realm (what we might call a "horizontal causality"). On this conception our realm is intrinsically fuzzy and volatile. Parmenides suggests

---

78. I owe this observation to Rogers Albritton.

79. On this construal, the "So" at the beginning of the third paragraph (132a10) should be regarded as inferential. See n. 46 above.

that this is what our world is like if physical objects do not participate in forms. Since Socrates lacks an account of participation that avoids Parmenides' objections, he has no answer to give to the objector who claims that there is no participation and hence that forms are unknowable. That is why Parmenides speaks of the final argument as the greatest difficulty.

Transition to Part II (134e–137c)

Why Are Forms Needed? (134e–135c)

By the end of the final argument in Part I it appears that forms, if they exist, have no relation to us, or we to them. So they are not responsible for the characters things have in our perceptible realm. Perceptible things are determined as what they are by their relations to other things in our realm. And since we have no access to forms, but only to things that belong to our realm, we cannot appeal to forms to explain our judgments about our world or the relations among things within it. Instead, we must be satisfied with appearances and with our inaccurate means of judging what they are appearances of.

Imagine ourselves like the prisoners in the cave described in *Republic* VII (514a–520d). Our legs and necks bound, we can observe only the shadows on the wall before us. We judge the appearances by comparing them with each other. There is, however, a crucial difference between the situation of the prisoners in the cave and our own at the end of the final argument in *Parmenides* Part I. For the prisoners in the cave, the shadows are cast by puppets being carried along the road in the firelight behind them. For the prisoners there is the possibility of a release from chains, of turning their vision away from the shadows and first observing the puppets themselves in the light of the fire, of then making their way out of the cave and ultimately beholding forms in the light of the form of the good. For them there is the possibility of returning to the cave and observing the shadows once more but now in the light of what they have learned. So for them there is the possibility of knowing the appearances and what they are appearances of.[80] For us there

---

80. See *Republic* 520c–d.

is no such possibility, since there is no way out of the cave. Although the shadows are cast by interacting objects, our only access to the objects is via the shadows. We have no fixed criteria by which to explain our judgments, and even if there were such criteria, they would be irrelevant, since the causal link between forms and appearances has been removed.[81] The world we are left with at the end of the final argument is intrinsically unstable.

This is a world we find three times described in the upcoming deductions in Part II: twice it is a world one can get no adequate grip on, once it is no world at all. Deduction 4 (159b–160b) describes a situation resembling that in the final argument in Part I: We are to imagine a situation in which the one exists but has no relation to other things. The one and the others are separate from each other both in the sense that they exist apart and in the sense that they are ontologically independent. According to the fourth deduction, since other things do not partake of the one, they cannot partake of any other determinate character either. In Deduction 7 (164b–165e) we are asked to imagine what other things would be like if there were no oneness. Here we have a world that exhibits vivid appearances, and we seem able to use those appearances to identify and differentiate things in relation to each other. Yet always on closer inspection we find that what we thought we saw is in fact a mirage. What gave rise to one impression suddenly gives rise to another. This is not merely a problem with our knowledge. The problem infects the things themselves, which keep dissolving before our eyes. By the eighth and final deduction (165e–166c) we discover that even the appearances have vanished: If the one is not, there is nothing at all (166c). This, in the end, is the cost of denying the existence of forms.

With this vision of what is at stake if forms are removed, Parmenides points out at the end of Part I that, despite all the difficulties that have just been discussed and a host of others besides, there must be forms. Otherwise we won't have anywhere to turn our thought and will destroy the power of dialectic entirely.[82] The question, then, is what to do about philosophy,

---

81. On p. 49 above I spoke of this causal link as "vertical" causality.

82. The word "dialectic" translates *dialegesthai*, which can also be translated as "discourse" or simply as "conversation." Since Parmenides here

while these difficulties remain unresolved. Socrates is now at a
loss and can make no suggestion.

That, says Parmenides, is because he has posited forms too
soon, before he has been properly trained.

The Exercise (135c–136a)

Three times over in the transitional section Parmenides insists
that training is a prerequisite for grasping the truth (135d; 136c;
136e). What is this truth? Its mention calls to mind the first part
of the poem by the historical Parmenides, and the two paths of
inquiry there described—the path of persuasion, which he said
attends upon Truth, that it is and cannot not be; and the other
path, which he said must be rejected as indiscernible, that it is
not and must not be.[83] Even so, the exercise Plato's Parmenides
now describes differs considerably from the path prescribed by
the historical Parmenides.

First, he says that the manner of the exercise is just what
Socrates heard from Zeno (135d). Recall that Zeno would start
with a hypothesis, contrary to Parmenides' own, that things are
many. He would then show that, if things are many, they have
incompatible properties. They are, for instance, both like and
unlike. Since the same things cannot have incompatible properties, the argument showed that the original hypothesis must be
rejected.

Second, Parmenides says that he was also impressed by something Socrates said to Zeno (135d–e). Whereas Zeno showed the
compresence of opposites in the case of visible things, Socrates
challenged him to display the same difficulty in the case of things
that are grasped by reasoning, which he called forms.[84] Notice
that in recalling Socrates' challenge, Parmenides does not commit

---

speaks of the "power of *dialegesthai*," it seems likely that he is talking
about a method that aims at uncovering the truth, not just ordinary
conversation. Plato characterizes *dialektike* in different ways in different
places: see *Republic* VI, 509d–511e and *Sophist* 253b–e. From what Parmenides goes on to say in the transitional section, it seems likely that
the exercise in Part II is an instance of *dialektike*, since he promises that
its reward will be a view of the truth.

83. See above pp. 8–10.

84. See the end of Socrates' long speech (129d–130a).

himself to what the objects are that we will reason about in the exercise. He says: "You asked him to observe it [the wandering between opposites] instead among those objects that one might above all grasp by means of reason and *might think* to be forms" (135e). Remember, too, that Parmenides has just reproved Socrates for positing forms too soon, before he has been properly trained (135c). The training certainly has implications for forms. Indeed we can even think of the objects discussed in Part II as forms.[85] Even so, the puzzles in Part I, whatever else they achieved, should at least have convinced us that we have no accurate insight into what forms are like. Many of the arguments and claims in Part II are peculiar, but if we approach this part of the dialogue with preconceptions about the status of its objects, we are likely to find it even more peculiar than it actually is.[86] Think of the objects in Part II—both the subjects of the deductions and the properties attributed to or denied of them— as entities we can reason about; think of them as forms if you like, but set aside whatever you thought you knew about Platonic forms.

Parmenides adds a third point to his description of the exercise. Whereas Zeno in his book started from a single hypothesis and derived various consequences, Parmenides says that Socrates must not only hypothesize that something is; he must also hypothesize that that same thing is not (135e–136a). Thus, whereas Zeno focused on the hypothesis of Parmenides' opponents, that things are many, and showed the absurd consequences that followed from that, Parmenides now recommends that we also consider the negation of that hypothesis, which Zeno endorsed, that things are not many, and examine the consequences that follow from that.

85. Deduction 2 mentions the one and the others and largeness and smallness as forms (149e), Deduction 3 mentions the one as a form (158c), and Deduction 4 speaks of likeness and unlikeness as forms (159e–160a).

86. Some examples: We expect forms not to be located in space, but in Deduction 2 the one has a location (145b–e); we expect forms to be unchanging and not in time, but again in Deduction 2 the one is in time and gets older and younger than itself and other things (151e–155c); we expect forms to be imperceptible, but Deduction 2 announces that the one is perceptible (155d).

This is a remarkable volte-face from the procedure the historical Parmenides advocated in his poem. He said that the path of not-being is indiscernible, and that no one could take it. Plato's Parmenides says that we are to take it and give it as much attention as we give to the opposing hypothesis. The proposal also indicates a change of policy from what we see in most other Platonic dialogues.[87] In discussions led by Socrates, someone proposes a thesis, often of the pattern "x is F," and Socrates examines it, typically with fatal consequences for the thesis. Only occasionally does he start again, taking the opposing thesis, "x is not F," and examine the consequences of that. Now the policy is that equal attention is to be given to both sides of an issue.[88]

Plan of the Deductions (136a–b)

Puzzled by Parmenides' third point (135e–136a), Socrates asks for clarification, and Parmenides offers an illustration. Before we look at that illustration, let us ask ourselves what we expect, given what he has already said. We expect the exercise to have two parts, starting from two opposed hypotheses. According to Parmenides' third prescription, these are: (1) if F is, and (2) if F is not. Within each of (1) and (2), we expect to see a series of arguments like those Zeno used: (1) if F is, F is both G and not-G, for various values of "G"; and (2) if F is not, F is both G and not-G, again for various values of "G." We have so far been led to expect two deductions, one starting from the positive hypothesis and one starting from the negative hypothesis. But when Parmenides illustrates the method, using Zeno's hypothesis, it appears to be more complicated:

87. There are some exceptions. See esp. the *Sophist*, which presents puzzles about both not-being and being (237b–251a). Of course, the *Sophist* refers back to the *Parmenides* (217c) and may have learned a lesson from it. But cf. also *Meno* 86d–96d on whether virtue is teachable, and the discussion of friends in the *Lysis*.

88. We have been prepared for the opposing arguments already in the *Parmenides*. Recall 128c–d, where Zeno says that Parmenides' opponents took Parmenides' hypothesis "if it is one" and derived absurd and contradictory consequences from it, and that Zeno himself took their hypothesis, "if it is many," and showed that the consequences on that hypothesis are even more absurd. The difference now is that the same person will examine both sides of the issue.

"If many are, what must the consequences be both for the many themselves in relation to themselves and in relation to the one, and for the one in relation to itself and in relation to the many? And, in turn, on the hypothesis, if many are not, you must again examine what the consequences will be both for the one and for the many in relation to themselves and in relation to each other." (136a–b)

The first point to notice is that, contrary to what we expected, Parmenides' illustration suggests that, starting from each hypothesis, we are to consider the consequences both for the entity (or entities) hypothesized (in this case the many) and for something else (in this case the one). Furthermore, whichever of the two we derive consequences for, we are to consider the consequences for it (them) in relation to itself (themselves) and in relation to the other entity (entities). How many parts of the positive and negative deductions does Parmenides envisage?

If we turn with this question in mind to the actual demonstration in Part II, which makes hypotheses about the one, we find a total of not two or four or eight deductions but—surprisingly—nine. On closer inspection this anomaly is not as troubling as one might initially think. In Part II four deductions start from the positive hypothesis, if one is, and four from the negative hypothesis, if one is not. In addition, there is a deduction that follows the second, which starts not from the original positive hypothesis but from the hypothesis that the one is what it was shown to be in the first and second deductions—both one and many (Deduction 2), and neither one nor many (Deduction 1), and (contrary to Deduction 1 but in conformity with Deduction 2) in time. We can therefore regard this deduction as an appendix to Deductions 1 and 2, and not part of the overall scheme described at the outset. Each of the two major deductions, starting from the positive or negative hypothesis, has four deductions as parts, for a total of eight deductions.

Why are there four deductions for each hypothesis rather than two or one? The reason for two deductions is evident both from the illustration about Zeno's hypothesis and from the actual strategy of Part II. For each of the positive and negative hypotheses, consequences are derived for the one or for the "others."[89]

---

89. What these "others" are is never made plain. Occasionally they are referred to as "the things not-one" (146d–147b). Think of them as entities

But there are two deductions treating each alternative. Why?[90]
Examination of the deductions themselves indicates that one
of each pair reaches positive conclusions, the other negative
conclusions for the same subject.[91] Thus, for example, the first
deduction, which starts from the positive hypothesis and examines consequences for the one, reaches negative conclusions
about it, whereas the second deduction reaches positive conclusions about it. Similarly, the third deduction reaches positive
conclusions about the others, whereas the fourth reaches negative conclusions about them. The conclusions of the paired deductions conflict with each other.

The scheme in Part II contains a number of anomalies. I have

---

other than the one. In Part II these appear to include largeness,
smallness, likeness, unlikeness, motion, rest, and the other entities that
apply or do not apply to the one. They may also include all entities we
can reason about, whether or not they are explicitly mentioned in Part II.

90. Constance Meinwald (1991) has proposed that one of each pair
considers the consequences for the subject (one, others) "in relation to
itself" (*pros heauto*), whereas the other considers consequences for the
same subject "in relation to the others" (*pros ta alla*), and she believes
the whole eightfold scheme is described in the illustration about Zeno's
hypothesis (cf. Sayre 1978, 136–37). According to Meinwald, these two
phrases introduce two types of predication, which will solve the main
puzzles in Part I (for a summary of that application, see Meinwald 1992).
But even if Meinwald is right that Part II distinguishes two types of
predication, she is in my view mistaken that the phrase "in relation to"
(*pros* with the accusative) is used in Part II to mark it out. The phrase
occurs often, but as she recognizes (177–78 n.2) exceedingly rarely in
the way that her thesis demands. In fact it is so used in just two instances
(161b, 161d), both of which she takes to be *pros ta alla*. We should be
guided by Parmenides' regular usage in interpreting the illustration
about Zeno. When Parmenides wants to say that an object A stands in
a certain relation to itself or other things (e.g., A is the same as itself,
different from other things, etc.), he typically says that A *has* the relation
(e.g., sameness, difference) *in relation to* (*pros*) itself and/or *in relation to*
(*pros*) other things (e.g., "the one has likeness in relation to itself," "the
one has inequality in relation to the others"). Since both options (in
relation to self/in relation to others) are treated in the same deductions,
the illustration about Zeno marks out four, not eight, alternatives.

91. Not all interpreters would agree with the claim that pairs of deductions treat the same subject. See p. 63 and n.105 below.

already mentioned the Appendix to the first and second deductions. Another irregularity is that the first deduction starts with a variant of the hypothesis. Whereas Deductions 2–4 start from the hypothesis "if one is," the first starts from what Parmenides describes as his own hypothesis, "if it is one" (137b).[92] Moreover, the order of the first and second deductions is reversed relative to that of the other six (whereas the consequences of the first deduction are negative, those of the second positive, the order of the other pairs is positive-negative).

Other variations are indicated in the following scheme, which provides a basic guide to the deductions. "F," "G," "H" stand for various features: one, many, whole, in time, knowable, perceptible. "R" and "not-R" stand for relational opposites, such as same and different, like and unlike, and equal and unequal. In the case of these, the subject is argued to be R and not-R (or neither R nor not-R) in relation to itself and/or other things (notice subtle variations indicated in this part of the scheme). In my outline I treat (3)/(4), (5)/(6), (7)/(8) as pairs, but I separate (1) and (2), because the hypothesis in the first deduction is given a distinct translation in English:

(1) If it is one, what follows for the one in relation to itself and in relation to the others?

   The one is not F, G, H, and it is neither R nor not-R in relation to either itself or the others.

(2) If one is, what follows for the one in relation to itself and in relation to the others?

   The one is F, G, H, and it is both R and not-R in relation to both itself and the others.

Appendix: If the one is as characterized in (1) and (2), and it is in time, what follows for it?

   The one is both F and not-F at different times, and so must change. At the instant of change it is neither F nor not-F.

(3)/(4) If one is, what follows for the others in relation to the one and in relation to themselves?

---

92. This anomaly will be explained below in the section entitled "The Positive Hypothesis."

(3) The others are F, G, H, and they are both R and not-R in relation to themselves and each other.

(4) The others are not F, G, H, and they are neither R nor not-R in relation to the one.

(5)/(6) If one is not, what follows for the one in relation to itself and in relation to the others?

(5) The one is F, G, H, and it is R and not-R in relation to either itself or the others.

(6) The one is not F, G, H, and it is neither R nor not-R in relation to either itself or the others.

(7)/(8) If one is not, what follows for the others in relation to the one and in relation to themselves?

(7) The others are F, and they are R in relation to each other; they also appear to be F, G, H, and R and not-R in relation to themselves and each other.

(8) The others neither are nor appear to be F, G, H, and they neither are nor appear to be R or not-R in relation to themselves or each other.

If we ignore the variations indicated in the scheme, the simple structure of the deductions (excluding the Appendix) can be seen in the following table (+ means positive, − negative):[93]

Deduction	Hypothesis	Subject	Consequences
1	+	one	−
2	+	one	+
3	+	others	+
4	+	others	−
5	−	one	+
6	−	one	−
7	−	others	+
8	−	others	−

This bare scheme suggests a repetitive strategy across deductions. The suggestion should be resisted. Part II is highly system-

93. A more detailed analysis of the deductions in Part II follows this introduction. For a helpful map of Part II, which sets out premisses of the arguments, see Owen 1970.

atic, but it also displays a striking progression, with later deductions criticizing or building on conclusions of previous ones. For instance, Deduction 2 opens by reassessing the meaning of the original hypothesis and by disputing the most dubious conclusion in Deduction 1;[94] the Appendix tries to reconcile the conclusions of Deductions 1 and 2; and Deduction 3 integrates the two perspectives to reach a number of constructive conclusions. Despite its peculiarity, Part II is very carefully crafted, with no sheer repetition.[95] Every argument of every deduction has something new to reveal. Deductions 3–8, though much shorter than Deductions 1 and 2, are at least as, if not more, provocative.

Aim of the Exercise (136b–c)

So far we have discussed Parmenides' recommendations for the exercise, his illustration of the method at 136a–b, and its application in Part II. Parmenides makes one further recommendation in response to Socrates' request for clarification. After he illustrates the procedure using Zeno's hypothesis, he points out (136b–c) that the method should be repeated, with other entities taken as subject. For example, Socrates should also hypothesize, if likeness is or if it is not, and examine the consequences on each hypothesis for likeness itself in relation to itself and in relation to the others, and for the others in relation to likeness and in relation to themselves and each other. The same method applies to unlikeness, to motion, to rest, to generation and destruction, and to being itself and not-being. In short, he says, the same method applies to whatever we might hypothesize as being or not being or as having any other property. This extension of the method is not demonstrated in Part II, which restricts itself to examining just one hypothesis and its negation.

Why does Parmenides recommend repeating the exercise with positive and negative hypotheses about different entities? Evi-

---

94. Namely, the conclusion that the one is not. See 141e–142a and 142b–c.

95. Whenever there would be repetitive reasoning, Parmenides leaves out the argument. For instance, in Deduction 2 he argues at length that the one is both like and unlike the others (147c–148d, discussed below, pp. 80–85), but then simply states that he could show in the same way that the one is like and unlike itself (148d).

dently the recommendation has some bearing on our unanswered question about the truth he keeps mentioning, because he concludes his description of the exercise by saying: "All this you must do if, after completing your training, you are to achieve a full view of the truth" (136c).

A similar methodological recommendation occurs in the *Meno*, with a similar forecast about its reward. In the middle of that dialogue (82b–85b) Socrates leads one of Meno's slaves through a geometrical demonstration. The problem is to determine on what base to construct a square twice the size of a four-foot square. Like the youthful Socrates in the first part of the *Parmenides*, Meno's boy at first thinks he knows the answers to questions about the geometrical problem and is repeatedly shown to be mistaken. He finally admits (again like Socrates in our dialogue, 135c) that he does not know what he thought he knew (*Meno* 84a). As Socrates points out in the *Meno*, the boy, stung by the recognition that he does not know, will now be glad to look for the answer (84b). In the second part of the geometrical exercise the boy works out the correct solution in response to Socrates' questions, locating the base of the eight-foot square on the diagonal bisecting the four-foot square.

At the end of the exercise Socrates says to Meno:

> "And these opinions have just now been stirred up in him like a dream. But if someone asks him about the same problem many times and in many ways, you know that he will have knowledge about these matters as accurate as anyone's." (85c–d)

Although the boy now has the correct answer to the geometrical problem, his answer does not yet constitute knowledge. Nonetheless his true judgment can be transformed into knowledge if someone repeats the exercise with him on numerous occasions and formulates the problem in different ways. The point of the repetition and variation is presumably to allow the boy to see the same problem displayed in various contexts, so that he can work out for himself why the answer is correct.[96]

Whatever the truth is that is to reward the student who masters the exercise in Part II of the *Parmenides*, together with its varia-

---

96. Cf. *Meno* 98a: True judgments are converted into knowledge by reasoning out the cause (*aitias logismos*).

tions, it is likely to be much more fundamental and abstract than is the truth that grounds the geometrical construction in the *Meno*. Even so, the analogy with the simpler case is instructive. In both cases the crucial point of repeating the exercise and reformulating the problem is to enable one, not simply to solve the problem, but to grasp the underlying principles that ground the solution. To gain this understanding from the exercise in the *Parmenides*, one must work through the entire exercise and repeat it starting from different hypotheses. Only then will one get the reward: a full view of the truth.

The Respondent (136c–137c)

Not surprisingly, Socrates still finds Parmenides' description obscure, and he now asks for a demonstration. After a good deal of hesitation Parmenides agrees and proposes to start with himself and his own hypothesis. He will hypothesize about the one itself and consider the consequences, "if it is one or if it is not one" (137b). This description alerts us to the fact that Deduction 1 will start from the variant hypothesis: "if it (the one) is one."

Parmenides selects Aristotle to be his interlocutor. Since Aristotle is the youngest person present, Parmenides says that he will cause the least trouble and be the most likely to say what he thinks. One suspects that the real reason for switching from Socrates to Aristotle is that Plato wants someone who will not interfere with the course of Parmenides' argument by raising interesting objections. Throughout Part II Parmenides maintains strict control of the proceedings. One might wonder why he bothers with an interlocutor at all, since the respondent has nothing of substance to contribute.[97] But giving a long speech would be highly inappropriate, because the upcoming demonstration has been introduced as an exercise for students. The respondent is therefore an essential part of the demonstration.[98]

97. F. M. Cornford in his well-known translation (1939, reprinted in Plato, *Collected Dialogues*) simply dispensed with Aristotle and turned the whole of Part II into a speech.

98. Some scholars, e.g., Brumbaugh 1961, take Aristotle's replies to indicate the structure of the arguments in Part II. For that reason we have been faithful in our translation of Aristotle's replies, except in a few instances where consistency could not be preserved (*Pōs d'ou?* is everywhere translated as "Doubtless," except at 139d1, where it must

At the same time his answers will, as Parmenides says, give him (and us) a chance to catch our breath.

It is worth asking what exercise Socrates is expected to perform on future occasions. Like us, he is a witness to the present demonstration, but next time he is to engage in the exercise himself. Is he to do what Parmenides does in Part II? Or what Aristotle does? Is he to be Parmenides to a less compliant Aristotle? Or a more critical Aristotle? Or is he to play the part of both in his own thinking? My own conjecture is that, until he has mastered the message (at which time he can take over the role of Parmenides), he is to be a more critical Aristotle.[99] I take it that this is also our own role in the upcoming exercise.

PART II (137c–166c)

Part II of the *Parmenides* is notoriously baffling.[100] Parmenides deduces an array of odd consequences for the one and the others. What is the one? What are the others? The entities under discussion are so elusive, and their properties and relations so abstract, that it is hard to fathom the point of the exercise. Moreover, attentive readers, especially if they have training in logic, will notice that some of the arguments contain blatant fallacies. A natural response, once one has made this observation, is simply to ignore Part II as a waste of time.

Some scholars of Plato, too, have had that reaction, though the historian is expected to have a story to tell. One proposal

---

be a proper question: "Why not?" *Pē dē?* is translated as "In what way?" at 154c6, 157c2, and 158e2, but as "Why is that?" at 165a7 and 165c6–7).

99. See 135a–b, where Parmenides says: "Only a very gifted man can come to know that for each thing there is some kind, a being itself by itself; but only a prodigy more remarkable still will discover that and be able to teach someone else who has sifted all these difficulties thoroughly and critically for himself." Socrates is plainly a gifted man who can come to know about forms. He is also someone who can sift difficulties thoroughly and critically for himself. But he is not (or at least not yet) the prodigy who can teach someone else.

100. For a useful survey of some older interpretations of the second part of the *Parmenides*, see Runciman 1959, 167–76.

from earlier in this century was that Plato's aim in Part II was to parody other philosophers by using arguments like theirs. On that view the arguments are not valid, nor did Plato think they were.[101] If Part II is a parody, full of invalid arguments, it is justifiably left to the specialists. But some eminent twentieth-century philosophers have read Part II and had a quite different reaction. Bertrand Russell called it "perhaps the best collection of antinomies ever made."[102] And Gilbert Ryle, in a famous paper on the dialogue, argued that it is an early essay in the theory of types.[103] Remember that in the transition to Part II Plato has Parmenides repeat three times that the exercise will give the student a view of the truth. The second part of the dialogue has an important message, though we must work hard to see it.

Some interpreters of Part II think that all or most of its arguments are valid.[104] One way to defend this claim is to argue that pairs of positive and negative deductions concern different entities. For instance, Deduction 1 has been taken to be about a one that is only one, and Deduction 2 to be about a one that is.[105] Another way to defend the claim is to argue that when two

---

101. Burnet 1914, 263–64; Cherniss 1932; Taylor 1934, 10–11, 39–40.

102. Russell 1937, 355. An antinomy is a contradiction between conclusions of arguments that seem equally reasonable.

103. Ryle 1939. In speaking of the theory of types, Ryle no doubt intended to call to mind Russell's solution to the contradiction sometimes known as the Russell Paradox (on one version: Is the class of all classes that are not members of themselves a member of itself? If it is, it isn't; if it isn't, it is). But in speaking of type-mistakes in the *Parmenides*, Ryle was interested in what he called "formal concepts" (concepts empty of content), which are modes of combining terms. According to Ryle, these are misused in Part II as though they were "proper concepts" (concepts with content), which are the terms to be combined in a proposition.

104. E.g., Cornford 1939, 107; Lynch 1959, 102; Sayre 1978; and Meinwald 1991, 19–27. A critique of Cornford's reading is given by Robinson 1953, 268–74.

105. Cornford 1939; Miller 1986, 96–99. Cf. Sayre 1978, 1983 (on Sayre's view Deductions 1 and 2 treat different subjects, but Deduction 1 is paired with Deduction 6, and Deduction 2 with Deduction 5, and these paired deductions treat the same subject). The first extant interpretation of this sort is that of the Neoplatonists, who took the first deduction to be about the One beyond being; the second about the second hypostasis,

deductions conflict, one considers what the subject is in virtue of its own nature, whereas the other considers what it is in virtue of natures other than its own.[106] These alternatives deserve serious consideration by readers of Part II.

In my view Part II contains some invalid arguments,[107] and many of the valid arguments rely on false premisses. Although Plato probably made some mistakes, most of the errors seem quite deliberate. Indeed, at the end of Deduction 1 Parmenides appears to announce that we should not accept all conclusions. Deduction 1 has shown that the one not only lacks other properties and relations, it even lacks being, and so neither is nor is one. Parmenides says: "But, as it seems, the one neither is one nor is, if we are obliged to trust this argument" (141e–142a). He goes on to say that since the one is not, it has no name or account. There is no knowledge, perception, or opinion of it. He ends the deduction by asking: "Is it possible that these things are so for the one?" And Aristotle replies: "I certainly don't think so" (142a). Parmenides casts doubt on the argument in Part II just this once, but once is enough to warn us that we are meant to beware.[108]

As I understand Part II, it highlights conflicts by means of antinomies and exposes errors based on invalid reasoning or misconceptions, and it challenges us, as readers, to notice what has gone wrong. My suggestion is that unlike the malleable young Aristotle, who expresses serious misgivings just once,

---

Nous; the third (which we have designated an appendix) about the third hypostasis, Soul; and so on. See Proclus, *Commentary on Plato's Parmenides*. On the Neoplatonic view, see Dodds 1928.

106. Meinwald 1991.

107. An obvious example of invalid reasoning is the pair of arguments in Deduction 2 that purport to show that the one is both at rest and in motion (145e–146a). Both rely on equivocations (cf. the meaning of "in the same thing" and "in a different thing" in these arguments and in the preceding section, 145b–e). Very often an invalid argument is quite unnecessarily so. See p. 81 and n.134 below for an example.

108. For interpretations of the end of Deduction 1 very different from my own, see Proclus, *Commentary on Plato's Parmenides* 63K–76K; Lynch 1959, 79–93; and Forrester 1972. Finding a plausible interpretation of this passage is crucial for those who want to hold that all the conclusions of Part II are acceptable.

and that only when prompted at the end of Deduction 1, we are meant to balk repeatedly and to respond. The exercise encourages us to recognize and diagnose the difficulties and to work out for ourselves what solutions are called for and why.

Readers of the second part of the *Parmenides* have hoped to find a single key that will unlock all its secrets.[109] I too think that there is one main issue that drives the deductions, but knowing what it is will prove more useful in unraveling Part II in light of its ending than in interpreting arguments along the way. For that reason we shall wait until the end of this introduction to discuss it. The most important thought to bring to Part II is that the deductions build upon one another. The primary aim of this introduction is to display that progression.

The One

The Positive Hypothesis (137c and 142b–c)

Parmenides sometimes expresses the positive hypothesis as *ei hen estin* (Deduction 1) and sometimes as *hen ei estin* (Deduction 2). Word order in English often affects the meaning of a sentence. Since Greek is an inflected language, the order of the words need not affect the meaning.[110] On the other hand, the Greek in both versions is underdetermined: *hen* ("one") is an adjective and can be construed either as subject or predicate in the hypothesis. Whether it is subject or predicate is highly significant for the meaning. Since the same ambiguity cannot be preserved in English, the translator must decide whether the appropriate translation is "if one is" or "if it is one." Evidence from the *Parmenides* itself suggests that the hypothesis in the first deduction should be translated as "if it (the one) is one," and in the

---

109. E.g., Ryle (1939) took Part II to expose errors about items of different logical types. Meinwald (1991) takes it to spell out a distinction between two sorts of predication. McCabe (1994, ch. 4) thinks it explores two conceptions of individuals. Although most of the keys help in interpreting the deductions, the disadvantage of keys is that Part II (and especially Deductions 3–8) tends to get distorted to fit them.

110. For a list of the different Greek forms of the positive and negative hypothesis in Part II, see Ross 1953, 92–93.

second and following deductions as "if one is." To see why, we must first return to Part I.

At the beginning of Part I Socrates mentions Zeno's and Parmenides' hypotheses and the hypothesis that Zeno denies, and he treats "one" and "many" as predicates. At 127e Socrates states that Zeno denies the hypothesis: "if things are many" (*ei polla esti ta onta*). Here a subject *ta onta* (literally, "the things that are") is explicitly mentioned, and "many" is the predicate. Again at 128a–b Socrates says that Parmenides claims that "the all is one" (*hen einai to pan*). Here too a subject, "the all," is explicitly mentioned, and "one" is the predicate. As the discussion proceeds, the subjects are not explicitly mentioned, but are presumably to be supplied from the preceding context. Thus at 128d Zeno states Parmenides' hypothesis in a form we recognize from Part II: *ei hen estin*. This is naturally translated as "if it (the all) is one," on the basis of Socrates' earlier statement of Parmenides' claim at 128a–b. At 128d Zeno also states the hypothesis that he denies as *ei polla estin*. Again "many" is naturally taken as the predicate in accordance with Socrates' original statement of that hypothesis at 127e. The opening part of the dialogue thus leads us to expect "one" and "many" to be predicates in the hypotheses of Part II.

Now consider Parmenides' prescriptions for the upcoming exercise in the transitional section. Recall that he said that the exercise is to be just what Socrates heard from Zeno, except that Socrates is to focus on objects that can be reasoned about rather than on visible things. Furthermore, whereas Zeno started from a single hypothesis and derived various consequences, Socrates must hypothesize not only "if each thing is" (*ei estin hekaston*) and consider the consequences, but also "if that same thing is not" (*ei me esti to auto touto*) (135e–136a). Here "each thing" and "that same thing" specify the subject of the positive and negative hypotheses and not the predicate. Next Parmenides illustrates the method using the hypothesis that Zeno denies and the one he endorses (136a–b). The Greek of the positive and negative hypotheses is underdetermined: *ei polla esti* and *ei me esti polla*. The proper construal is determined by Parmenides' prescription directly preceding. Since he said that Socrates must first hypothesize, if each thing is, and then hypothesize, if that same thing is not, "many" in the illustration should be construed accordingly. So "many" is the subject of the hypothesis, and the positive

and negative hypotheses are "if many are" and "if many are not." This construal gains support a few lines later, when Parmenides claims that we must repeat the exercise starting from the hypothesis "if likeness is" (*ei estin homoiotes*) (136b). Use of an abstract noun instead of an adjective suggests that "likeness" is the subject, not the predicate, in that hypothesis. Contrary to our observations about the early part of the dialogue, this evidence leads us to expect "one" and "many" to be subjects of hypotheses in the upcoming exercise.

There is one last piece of evidence from Part I. When Parmenides finally yields to the entreaties of his companions and agrees to go through the demonstration himself, he proposes that he will begin with himself and his own hypothesis. He says that he will hypothesize about the one itself and consider what the consequences must be "if it is one or if it is not one" (*eite hen estin eite me hen*) (137b). This translation, which takes "one" as predicate, is the only possible rendering of the Greek without emending the text.[111] We need feel no surprise that Parmenides states his own hypothesis this way, with "one" as predicate rather than subject, given Socrates' earlier characterization of his claim as "the all is one" (128a–b). "If it is one" simply follows from that formulation. This statement sets the stage for the hypothesis in Deduction 1 of Part II.

Although no subject is explicitly mentioned in the first hypothesis, the subject is clearly the one. Parmenides said that he would hypothesize about the one itself (137b). Furthermore, the opening sentence of the first deduction mentions the subject in the main clause of the sentence: "If it is one, *the one* would not be many" (137c). So the hypothesis in Deduction 1 should be understood as: "if it (the one) is one." This translation appears to be confirmed by Parmenides' last statement in the opening paragraph of Deduction 1: "Therefore, if *the one* is to be *one* (*ei hen estai to hen*), it will neither be a whole nor have parts" (137d). Here *hen* is predicate, and the subject of the hypothesis, the one (*to hen*), is explicitly mentioned.

---

111. Emendations have been proposed, so that *hen* can be construed as subject: either delete the final *hen* or replace it with *estin*. The emendation was proposed by Wundt 1935, 6, and has been adopted by Cornford 1939, 108, and Allen 1983, 15, and defended by Meinwald 1991, 39–45.

There is one further, crucial piece of evidence that should guide our construal of the hypothesis in the first and second deductions. At the beginning of Deduction 2 (142b1–c7), Parmenides discusses the meaning of the positive hypothesis and distinguishes two ways to understand it—as "if one is one"[112] and "if one is." He says that this time (in Deduction 2) it is to be construed as "if one is."[113] This passage strongly suggests both that the hypothesis in Deduction 1 should be construed as "if one is one" and that the hypothesis in Deduction 2 should be construed as "if one is."

Why does Parmenides take the hypothesis in different ways in Deductions 1 and 2? To answer that question, we must first ask what the hypothesis means in its two versions. In the hypothesis "if one is one," the "is" is an incomplete predicate which links the subject to the predicate that completes the clause. Since both the subject and the predicate are adjectives rather than nouns, we face a further question. Should we understand "is" as an identity-sign, as in the sentence "Socrates is the son of Sophroniscus"? In that case both the subject and the predicate are referring expressions, and the phrase that completes the predicate reidentifies the subject. Alternatively, should we understand the "is" as a sign of predication, as in the sentence "Simmias is large"? In that case only the subject is a referring expression, and the predicate describes the subject by ascribing a property to it. Given these options, we must ask: Is the hypothesis "one is one" an identity statement, or is it a predication? If the latter, it is a special sort of predication which we also encountered in Part I: a self-predication.

The first sentence of the first deduction gives us a reason to take the hypothesis as a self-predication: "If it is one, the one would not be many" (137c). Notice that the subject of the main clause is specified with a definite article ("the one") and that the

112. The Greek is *ei hen hen* (literally "if one one"), but the Greek verb "is" can be omitted when it functions as a copula, as it does here. For a different interpretation see Schofield 1973, 31–32.

113. Cf. Cornford 1939, 136 and note. Similar interpretations of the hypotheses in Deductions 1 and 2 are given by Taylor 1934, 64, 73, and Hardie 1936, 101–2.

predicate ("many") is specified without an article. Had Parmenides intended to state a non-identity (i.e., had he intended to claim that the one and the many are different things), he could have said: "the one would not be *the* many." Since there is a definite article with the subject-expression but not with the predicate, the main clause expresses a negative description, not a non-identity. Once we supply "the one" as subject for the hypothesis itself, the same consideration gives us grounds to take it as a self-predication, not a statement of identity. Parmenides is saying that if the one is one (i.e., has the character oneness), then it is not many (i.e., lacks the character multitude). This construal appears to be confirmed by Parmenides' last sentence in the first paragraph of Deduction 1: "if the one is to be one . . ." (137d). Use of the definite article with the subject expression but not with the predicate is a good indication that the hypothesis in Deduction 1 is a self-predication.[114]

In the version of the hypothesis in the second deduction, "if one is," the verb "to be" functions as a complete predicate: the clause requires nothing further to interpret the meaning. Since English has a separate verb "exists" which functions as a complete predicate, where Greek uses simply "is," many interpreters of the *Parmenides* have translated the hypothesis as "if one exists." This translation is misleading, because it suggests that the incomplete "is" we encountered in the first deduction and the complete "is" we encounter in the second deduction have different meanings. Consider the sentence: "Pegasus *is* a winged horse, but he does not *exist*." We make identity statements and predications about nonexistent objects. Only some objects we describe actually exist. So incomplete "is" and "exists" have different meanings in English. It is not at all clear that incomplete and complete "is" have different meanings for Plato.[115]

---

114. Identity statements occur as Parmenides' argument proceeds, as in the sentence: "Round *is* surely that whose extremities are equidistant in every direction from the middle" (137e). Here "that whose extremities are equidistant in every direction from the middle" reidentifies (in fact defines) "round." Cf. the statement of non-identity in Deduction 3 at 157b9: "the others are not the one" (*oute to hen esti talla*).

115. Cf. our discussion of the historical Parmenides above, p. 9.

Plato's use of the verb "to be" has been much debated, especially in discussions of the *Sophist*.[116] One question has been
whether the syntactically distinct uses in "A is B" and "A is"
indicate a semantic distinction between the incomplete "is" of
predication and the complete "is" of existence.[117] In a ground-
breaking study of Plato's *Sophist*, Lesley Brown has argued that
there is no sharp semantic distinction between the two uses.[118]
She contrasts two pairs of sentences.

　1a Jane is growing tomatoes.
　1b Jane is growing.
　2a Jane is teaching French.
　2b Jane is teaching.

In (1a) the verb "is growing" is transitive (i.e., takes a direct
object). Let us call it an incomplete use of the verb "is growing,"
since something further is required to complete the meaning. In
(1b) the verb "is growing" is intransitive (i.e., takes no direct
object), and we can call it a complete use of the verb "is growing,"
since it needs nothing further to complete the meaning. Indeed,
we have clearly misunderstood (1b) if we ask "is growing what?"
The intransitive use of "is growing" does not allow a further
completion. There is, then, a sharp semantic distinction between
(1a) and (1b) that corresponds to the syntactic distinction. Now
consider (2a) and (2b). Again the use of the verb "is teaching"
in (2a) is transitive, that in (2b) intransitive. But if someone says
"Jane is teaching," it is perfectly correct to ask "is teaching what?"
The use of "is teaching" in (2b) is complete as it stands but
allows further completion: if Jane is teaching, then she is teaching
something. Brown suggests that Plato's complete use of "is" in
"A is" is analogous with (2b). The "is" is complete but allows
further completion.[119]

---

116. For some important contributions to this debate, see Ackrill 1957,
Frede 1967 (summarized in English in Frede 1992), and Owen 1971.

117. Another question has been whether Plato distinguishes between
the "is" of identity and the "is" of predication, or between the "is" of
accidental predication and the "is" of essential predication. One attrac-
tive suggestion is that he uses "is" in a single sense everywhere: see
Mates 1979.

118. Brown 1986.

119. Brown 1986, 54–55.

This proposal illuminates the *Parmenides*, because in Part II Plato appeals to only one entity, being, in his analysis of both the incomplete and the complete uses of the verb "to be." At the end of Deduction 1 Parmenides says that the one cannot even "*be*" one (incomplete), because it would then, by being and *partaking of being*, be" (141e). At the beginning of Deduction 2, he asks: "if one *is* (complete), can it be, but not *partake of being*?" (142b). Since Parmenides appeals to the same entity—being— in both contexts, no semantic distinction is envisaged between "is" in its incomplete and complete uses. Had he intended a semantic distinction, he could have posited two entities to explicate the two senses.

These observations suggest that the complete "is" in Greek does not correspond to our modern notion of existence.[120] Plato evidently assumes that if x is F then x is.[121] So Pegasus is, since we can describe him. There is no harm in translating "is" in this context as "exists," if we recognize that many more things exist for Plato than exist for us. For him anything we can describe exists. Nonetheless, the advantage of using the same translation for the Greek verb "to be" in its complete and incomplete uses is that we are reminded that the same notion of being is at work in both contexts and also deterred from thinking that Plato shares our notion of existence.

The difference between the hypotheses in Deductions 1 and 2, then, is that the first hypothesis characterizes the one in a particular way, namely as being one, whereas the second leaves open precisely what the one is, hypothesizing only that the one is (something or other). Let us now consider the consequences Parmenides derives starting from the two versions of the positive hypothesis.

The First Antinomy: Deductions 1 (137c–142a) and 2 (142b–155e)

Deductions 1 and 2 both consider consequences for the one, but they reach conflicting conclusions. Deduction 1 starts from the

120. Charles Kahn has a series of papers that treat this topic. See esp. Kahn 1966, 1976, and 1986 (also cited above in n.10).

121. See Brown 1986, 69; cf. Owen 1970, 352 (his premiss 8), and Moravcsik 1982, 143, as well as Kahn's papers.

hypothesis "if the one is one," and demonstrates that the one is neither F nor not-F for various values of "F." Deduction 2 starts from the hypothesis "if one is," and demonstrates that it is both F and not-F for those same values. There is a conflict not only between the conclusions of Deductions 1 and 2 but also among some of the conclusions within Deduction 2.

The items treated in Part II include various properties, such as one and many, limited and unlimited, and motion and rest; and also various relations, such as same and different, like and unlike, and equal and unequal. Some of the properties and relations discussed in Part II should apply to everything. For instance, any object that can be named is one, has being, is the same as itself and different from other things. Others, such as motion and rest and equal and unequal, properly apply only to a specific range of objects. For instance, things subject to motion and rest have a spatial location and a temporal duration. Things that are equal or unequal can be somehow quantified: they have a size or duration that can be measured, or they are numerable, and so can be counted.

The first deduction defies our expectations about the universal applicability of properties like being and oneness, and of relations like sameness and difference. Here, starting from the hypothesis that the one is one, Parmenides demonstrates that the one is nothing at all—not even one. Most of the conclusions, though initially surprising, are in fact quite plausible, once we recognize that he is examining what the one is by itself, that is, solely in virtue of its oneness.

Consider the arguments Parmenides gives to show that the one is not different from anything else and not the same as itself. He argues that the one cannot be different from anything, because if it were, it would have to be so by difference, not by itself:[122]

> "And it won't be different from another, as long as it is one; for it is not proper to one to be different from something, but proper to different-from-another alone, and to nothing else."—"That's right."—"Therefore it won't be different by being one. Or do you

---

122. The commentaries by Cornford 1939 and Allen 1983 are worth consulting on any argument in Part II. This argument is also discussed by Meinwald 1991, 63–67.

think it will?"—"No indeed."—"Yet if it isn't different by being one, it will not be so by itself; and if it isn't so by itself, it will not itself be so. And if it is itself in no way different, it will be different from nothing."—"That's right." (139c)

He argues on similar grounds that the one is not the same as itself:[123]

"Nor will it be the same as itself."—"Why not?"—"The nature of the one is not, of course, also that of the same."—"Why?"—"Because it is not the case that, whenever a thing comes to be the same as something, it comes to be one."—"But why?"—"If it comes to be the same as the many, it must come to be many, not one."— "True."—"But if the one and the same in no way differ, whenever something came to be the same, it would always come to be one; and whenever it came to be one, it would always come to be the same."—"Certainly."—"Therefore, if the one is to be the same as itself, it won't be one with itself; and thus it will be one and not one. But this surely is impossible." (139d–e)

In these two arguments Parmenides contends that the nature of the different and the nature of the same differ from the nature of the one. So if the one is one in the very strong sense that the only features it has are those explained by its oneness, then it cannot be the same as or different from anything at all, because these features would be explained by natures other than its own.

These arguments rely on a thesis that we have encountered before, both in the *Phaedo* and in Part I of the *Parmenides*. Recall Socrates' "safe" explanation in the *Phaedo*. It is *by the beautiful* that many beautiful things are beautiful (100d). The beautiful itself is the cause of beauty in other things, and as a cause it has the character that other things have in virtue of it. Similarly, in the Largeness Regress in Part I of the *Parmenides*, it is *by largeness* that many large things are large (132a–b). And because the form of largeness is large, it can be grouped together with things that are large in virtue of it. In the same way Parmenides assumes in the first deduction in Part II that if something is different from anything, the cause of that difference is difference, and if something is the same as anything, the cause of that sameness

---

123. For alternative interpretations of this argument, see Schofield 1974, Curd 1989, 353–55, and Meinwald 1991, 86–91.

is sameness. So if the one were different from anything, it would be so *by difference*, and if it were the same as anything, it would be so *by sameness*. This causal thesis is maintained in the second deduction,[124] as well as the first, and reappears in the *Sophist*.[125] Whatever Plato thought of the criticisms of forms in Part I, the view that intelligible entities are causes is apparently one he found worth preserving.

The first deduction argues that whatever the one is it is *by itself*, that is, *by oneness*. Given that perspective, all that the one is by itself is one. Any other feature would be caused by a nature other than its own. By the end of the first deduction, however, Parmenides reveals that the one is not only not many, not located, not subject to motion and rest, not the same as anything, not different from anything, not like anything, not unlike anything, and so on: it is not even one.

How does Parmenides reach this remarkable conclusion? He argues that *to be* one, the one would have to partake of being. The argument he gives to show that the one does not partake of being rests on a misconception. He claims that the one would have to be in time to partake of being. He assumes, and young Aristotle agrees, that being is always tensed, that "was" indicates time past, "will be" indicates time hereafter, and "is" indicates time present. On this view, if the one partook of being, it would have to be in time—or as Parmenides says, it would have to come to be older or younger (141a; 151e–155d). According to the first deduction, the one does not come to be older or younger, and so is not in time. Since it is not in time, it does not partake of being. And so, he concludes, "neither *is* it in such a way as to be one, because it would then, by being and partaking of being, be" (141e).

Presumably the view that being is always tensed is one that

---

124. See 143b, where Parmenides argues that if one and being are different, they are different by difference; cf. 149e.

125. At *Sophist* 255e the Eleatic Visitor claims that the different pervades the other kinds and is responsible for the difference between them: "Indeed we shall say that it pervades all of them. For each one is different from the others, not because of its own nature, but because it partakes of the character of the different."

young Aristotle and the audience are meant to notice and question, because elsewhere Plato repudiates it. In the *Timaeus* he
has Timaeus explicitly say that the present tense of the verb "to
be" can be used to indicate eternal being. In that work Timaeus
describes the creation of time, which he calls the moving image of
eternity. In a passage reminiscent of our section of the *Parmenides*
(and of its counterpart in Deduction 2 [151e–155d]), Timaeus
says that past and future tenses are incorrectly applied to eternal
being, but that the present tense can be applied to it:

> All these [days and nights, months and years] are parts of time, and
> "was" and "will be" are forms of time that have come to be, which
> we incorrectly transfer, without noticing, to eternal being. For we
> say that it [eternal being] "was" and "is" and "will be." But according
> to the true account "is" alone properly applies to it, whereas "was"
> and "will be" are appropriately used for coming-to-be that proceeds
> in time, since they are motions. It is not proper for that which remains
> unchangingly the same to come to be either older or younger through
> time, nor to have come to be so in the past, or now, or to be so
> hereafter. (37e–38a)

According to this passage, "is" should remain available for statements about eternal, unchanging objects. So it should be acceptable to say "the one is one." In this self-predication, "is" is used
timelessly to ascribe to the one an essential property—a property
it must have to be what it is.[126]

Even if young Aristotle fell too easily into Parmenides' trap,
we are left with a puzzle at the end of the first deduction. If the
one is considered as what it is solely in virtue of itself, can it *be*
(timelessly) one without partaking of a character other than its
own? What is the function of being, which connects the one to
its character? Is it *by being* as well as *by oneness* that the one is
one? If so, then the conclusion of the first deduction stands. If
the one is considered as what it is solely in virtue of itself, it
cannot even be one.

The second deduction pursues the idea that being is a character

---

126. On Plato's treatment of time, see Owen 1966. One could also argue
that "is" in these contexts marks the eternal present. See Kahn 1966,
255–56.

distinct from oneness. As we have already observed, Parmenides begins by reassessing the original hypothesis, and he says that this time it will be construed as "if one is," not "if one is one" (142b–c). The question is, what are the consequences for the one if it partakes of being, a character distinct from its oneness? Whereas Deduction 1 considers what the one is solely in virtue of itself and concludes that it is nothing at all, Deduction 2 considers what it is in virtue of other things, giving no priority to what it is in itself. The one now turns out to be everything it failed to be in Deduction 1—one and many, the same as itself, the same as the others, different from the others, different from itself, and so on. Some of its features are incompatible with one another. The source of the trouble is that, since no priority is given to what the one is in its own right, its character keeps shifting within and across arguments. So viewed under one description it is F, but viewed under another description, it is not-F.

We as readers are invited to reflect on the conflicts both between the first and second deductions, and within the second deduction, and to ask what has gone wrong. Are the conclusions of one deduction to be accepted, those of the other rejected? Probably not. As we have already seen, Parmenides himself calls into question the conclusion of the first deduction (141e–142a). We cannot accept all conclusions of the second deduction either, since some of them conflict with each other. One possible moral is that, to make progress, we should integrate the perspectives of the two deductions: We should consider what an object is both in virtue of itself and in virtue of other things. Either perspective on its own apparently leads to absurdity—at one extreme to the object's being nothing at all, and at the other extreme to its being everything indiscriminately. If instead we combine the two perspectives, our knowledge of what a thing is by itself will determine, to a large extent, what other properties and relations can be ascribed to it.

As we shall see, Parmenides offers two ways to resolve the conflicts of Deductions 1 and 2, one in the Appendix, and one in Deduction 3. Before we examine those proposals, however, let us consider a selection of puzzles in the second deduction that exemplify Parmenides' strategy in Part II and have special bearing on Socrates' troubles in Part I.

One and Many (Deduction 2: 142c–145a)

In Part I Socrates introduced a theory of forms to resolve Zeno's contradictions about comprescent opposites. Socrates claimed that it was unproblematic that he himself is both one and many (129c–d). Someone could show that he is many by pointing out that his right side is different from his left, his front from his back, and similarly with his upper and lower parts. He is many, said Socrates, because he partakes of multitude. Someone could also show that he is one by pointing out that he is one person among the seven people present. That, he says, is because he partakes of oneness. Now what about the one itself? Is it also many? It was essential to Socrates' theory that forms themselves not be subject to the comprescence of opposites. For if they were, he would need to introduce further entities to explain the comprescence in them.

At the end of his long speech in Part I (129d–130a), Socrates challenged Parmenides to show that Zeno's problem about comprescent opposites is not restricted to visible things but infects intelligible objects as well. In the second deduction Parmenides gives two arguments that respond to that challenge. He argues twice that the one is many, in fact unlimited in multitude.[127]

According to Deduction 2, if one is, the one partakes of being. So there is the being of the one, which is not the same as the one (142b). In the first argument to show that the one is unlimited in multitude (142d–143a), Parmenides says that the hypothesis "if one is" indicates that the one has parts. Since the thing hypothesized, the one that is, is one being, it is a whole whose parts are oneness and being. Oneness and being are properties of the one, and they are here treated as its parts. Now consider each of the parts of the one being, oneness and being. Is being ever absent from the oneness part, or oneness from the being part? No: each part has two parts, oneness and being; and each of those parts has two parts, and so on indefinitely. The one that is is thus unlimited in multitude.

The second argument (143a–144e) focuses on the one itself,

---

127. The general implications of these arguments for Plato's later philosophy are discussed by Anscombe 1966. See also Schofield 1973, Allen 1974, and Curd 1990.

apart from the being it partakes of. Surely if the one is considered apart from its being, it will be one and not many? Not so. Since we are considering the one alone by itself, apart from being, we agree that one and being are different. What makes them different (143b)? Consistent with the causal thesis we discussed earlier,[128] Parmenides says that it is not by being one that the one is different from being, nor by being being that being is different from one. On the contrary, they are different from each other by difference, and difference is not the same as either of them. So we now have three distinct entities, oneness, being, and difference. We can think of any two of them—oneness and being, oneness and difference, or being and difference—and each pair will be two and each member of the pair one. We can add any one to any two, and get a total of three. Since we have two, we can take two twice and get four. And since we have three, we can take three three times and get nine. We can also take three two times or two three times and get six. Then we can manipulate our results and their results and end up with all the numbers.[129] Aren't all the numbers beings? So don't they each partake of being? Since they do, being is distributed to all of them, and the parts of being are countless.

Now think of all the parts of being. Each part is one part, so oneness is attached to each. Can the one, as a whole, be in many places at the same time? Young Aristotle, doubtless recalling the first side of the Whole-Part Dilemma from earlier in the day (130e–131e), immediately agrees that this is impossible. Parmenides concludes, as he did then, that the one is divided into parts and distributed to all the parts of being. So the one itself is unlimited in multitude, since it has an unlimited number of parts.

Both of these arguments show that the one is unlimited in multitude by revealing that it has an unlimited number of parts. The parts in the two arguments are of different types. In the

---

128. See above, pp. 34–35 and 73–74.

129. Scholars often point out that this argument fails to generate all the numbers, because it ignores the primes. This doesn't matter for the argument, since the aim is simply to produce an unlimited number of entities, and that is achieved even without the primes. Alternative interpretations of this argument are given by Cornford 1939, 141 n.2, Allen 1970, and Moravcsik 1982, 143–44.

first argument the one has an unlimited number of property-parts, though its property-parts are of just two sorts, oneness and being.[130] In the second argument, the one has an unlimited number of instance-parts.[131] As in the second side of the Whole-Part Dilemma in Part I, the one is like a quantity of stuff that is split up into parts and distributed to all the things that partake of it. On either conception of parts, the one is unlimited in multitude.

This section sets the stage for a whole series of puzzles in Deduction 2. Immediately following the second argument for unlimitedness, Parmenides says:

> "Furthermore, because the parts are parts of a whole, the one, as the whole, would be limited. Or aren't the parts contained by the whole?"—"Necessarily."—"But surely that which contains would be a limit."—"Doubtless."—"So the one that is is surely both one and many, a whole and parts, and limited and unlimited in multitude."—"Apparently." (144e–145a)

If the one is both one and many, both a whole and parts, and both limited and unlimited in multitude, it will have countless other incompatible features as well, as Deduction 2 goes on to demonstrate.

Not only do these two arguments set the stage for the rest of the second deduction, they also expose a serious problem for Socrates' theory of forms in Part I. If the one itself is both one and many, how can it account for the oneness of other things, as his theory requires? What accounts for its own oneness? Must there be a further one, which is simply one and not many? How can that one not be many, given these two arguments? The second one would also have an unlimited number of property-parts, as did the one in the first argument, and it would have

---

130. Compare this result with the treatment in the *Phaedo* of Simmias' largeness and smallness, as discussed above: his largeness and smallness are parts *of him*.

131. Compare this result with the treatment of forms in the Whole-Part Dilemma in Part I of the *Parmenides*: the instances of a form are parts *of it*. On the distinction between two sorts of parts, cf. Allen 1974, 701; Schofield 1977, 151; and Curd 1988, 315. I owe the labels "property-parts" and "instance-parts" to Harte 1994, 64–65.

even more instance-parts than did the one in the second argument, since that one is now an additional instance of it. So there would need to be a third one, and a fourth, and so on indefinitely. No ideal specimen of oneness will be found that is simply one. Reflection on this argument suggests that there will be an explanatory regress like that in the Largeness Regress in Part I: there is no ultimate oneness that can explain the oneness of other things, because each one is also many.

The problem of compresent opposites is not peculiar to oneness, but to all abstract objects that have universal application. Presumably the extensiveness of the problem of compresence is something that will become evident to anyone who follows Parmenides' recommendation and repeats the exercise starting from hypotheses about likeness, unlikeness, and other abstract objects (136b). One will realize that if these abstract entities apply to everything, they also apply to their own opposite. For instance, sameness is the same (as itself) but also different (from other things); difference is different (from other things) but also the same (as itself); likeness is like (itself) but also unlike (other things); unlikeness is unlike (other things) but also like (itself); being is (various things) but also is not (other things).[132] In the case of these objects at least—objects that Socrates presumably includes as forms at stage one of Parmenides' inquiry about the scope of forms in Part I—the compresence of opposites cannot be avoided. Since these objects are subject to compresence, there will inevitably be a regress if he insists that an object that explains the corresponding feature in other things cannot itself be subject to its own opposite.

Likeness and Unlikeness (Deduction 2: 147c–148d)

Occasionally Parmenides spotlights a shocking argument, but he never openly announces what has gone wrong. In Deduction 2 he gives an odd argument to show that the one is like the others, and then an astonishing argument, using the previous conclusion, to show that it is unlike the others (147c–148c). The arguments are peculiar in part because he ignores the strategy by which he established the opposite conclusions in Deduction

---

132. Cf. *Sophist* 254d–257a, where Plato analyzes such cases.

1 (139e–140b). There, having shown that the one is neither the same as nor different from another (139b–e),[133] he claimed that same entails like and different entails unlike, and concluded (invalidly) that the one is neither like nor unlike another.[134] In Deduction 2, having shown that the one is both the same as and different from the others (146a–147b), he could have used the assumption from Deduction 1 that same entails like and different entails unlike and this time reached a valid conclusion that the one is both like and unlike the others.

Instead of taking that straightforward route, he gives a tortuous argument from difference to likeness and from sameness to unlikeness. This strategy, though more blatant here than elsewhere, is typical of Parmenides' method in Part II: if there is an obvious route to a conclusion, he ignores it and arrives by a circuitous route instead. In our section on likeness and unlikeness, he signals the peculiarity of his arguments by giving two short new arguments for the very same conclusions, this time arguing from sameness to likeness and from difference to unlikeness to reach the valid conclusion that the one is both like and unlike the others (148c–d). It is as though he were saying: "Notice! What was wrong with what I just did?" More often we are left to catch mistakes for ourselves.

The challenge is not simply to notice errors but to diagnose them. We have already noticed that the second part of the *Parmenides* focuses on entities that are highly abstract. Unlike human being or animal, redness or color, justice or virtue—entities with determinate content, whether specific, like human being, redness, or justice; or generic, like animal, color, or virtue—most

---

133. In the section entitled "The First Antinomy" above, we considered two of Deduction 1's four arguments concerning sameness and difference, namely, that the one is not different from another (139c) and not the same as itself (139d–e). Parmenides also argued that it is not different from itself and not the same as another (139b–c).

134. The fallacy is that of denying the antecedent. Parmenides assumes that same entails like (139e8) and argues not same, so not like; he also assumes that different entails unlike (140a7–b1) and argues not different, so not unlike. He could easily have assumed that not same entails not like and that not different entails not unlike, and reached the same conclusions without the invalidity.

of the items treated in the second part of the dialogue lack deter-minate content.[135] The entities that Socrates embraced as forms at the first stage of Parmenides' inquiry about the scope of forms in Part I, such as one and many, and likeness and unlikeness, are properties or relations that apply to objects on the basis of other, ultimately determinate, properties they have. For exam-ple, two objects are equal or unequal if they have some definite size or duration, or if they are numerable. Two objects are like if they have one or more properties in common. Two objects are unlike if there is some property they do not share. Thus Simmias is like Socrates in various respects, and one of those respects is that they are both human beings. They are also unlike in various respects, and one of those respects is that Simmias has a determi-nate size that is not the same as Socrates' size. The application of the expressions "like" and "unlike" is very flexible. Two ob-jects are like if they have any feature in common, however gen-eral or abstract that feature. And two objects are unlike if they differ in any respect whatsoever.

This observation should indicate both why the first argument for likeness is odd and why it is nonetheless sound. The argu-ment is odd, because we expect two objects to be like on the basis of some determinate feature they share. If difference itself is viewed as a feature that can be shared, then any object is like any other, because every object is different from something.[136]

Young Aristotle is perplexed by the argument and asks for clarification (147c). Parmenides responds by explaining our use of names (147d–e). He says that each name we use applies to something, and that the same name applies to the same object, whether we use it once or more than once. To supply a concrete example, however often we use the name "Socrates, son of Sophroniscus," the name applies to the same person. Now ex-

---

135. There are some exceptions. For instance, motion (*kinesis*) is treated in Deduction 1 (138b–139a) and 5 (162b–e) as a generic notion, and it is divided into species, alteration and spatial motion (*phora*); spatial motion is further divided into sub-species, change of place and rotation.

136. Since "something" ranges over all objects, the one and the others can have the same property, even though the one is *different from the others* and the others are *different from the one*. They have the same property because both are *different from something*.

tend the point to the word "different." "Different," says Parmenides, is the name for something. Whether we use the name once or more than once, it always applies to that nature whose name it is. So if we say "the others are different from the one" and "the one is different from the others," although we use "different" twice, the name applies to the same object. To be sure, "different" does not operate as a referring expression in either sentence, as "Socrates, son of Sophroniscus" does in "Socrates, son of Sophroniscus, was the teacher of Plato." Even so, "different" specifies the same entity in both sentences, one that we can speak of either as *difference*—a relation between entities—or as *difference from something*—a relational property that each entity has. This clarification made, Parmenides repeats his previous point. Insofar as the one is different from the others, and the others different from it, on the basis of having difference in common, the one has the same property as the others, and they have the same property as it. Since things that have the same property are like, the one is like the others owing to their difference.

We now turn to the argument that the one and the others are unlike owing to their sameness. Whereas the first argument was odd but sound, this one is scandalous. The same consideration that applied in that argument should apply here too. If two objects have some feature in common, however abstract, they are like. So if the one and the others are the same as each other (a conclusion previously demonstrated [146d–147b]), they are like, because they have sameness in common. Notice that even in the preceding argument, where the one turned out to be like the others owing to their difference, it was because they had the *same* property—difference—that they turned out to be like. Sameness entails likeness.

Parmenides ignores that point, however, and introduces a different consideration. He contends that like is the opposite of unlike, and different the opposite of same. So, given the previous conclusion that the one and the others are like on the basis of their difference, he now contends that they are unlike on the basis of their sameness. Since difference grounds their likeness, its opposite, sameness, grounds their unlikeness. The strangeness of this conclusion reveals that something is seriously amiss in the conception of the abstract relations sameness and difference and likeness and unlikeness that Parmenides presents for young Aristotle's consideration.[137]

No doubt Parmenides expects his young interlocutor (and their audience) to be shocked by the conclusion, but this time Aristotle acquiesces without asking for clarification. Perhaps he is seduced by a false analogy. Parmenides appears to be treating sameness and difference as though they were determinate opposites, like justice and injustice. And he seems to be treating likeness and unlikeness as though they were genera, like virtue and vice. Justice, courage, piety, and so on are species of virtue; injustice, cowardice, impiety, and so on are species of vice. If one of the specific characters applies to an object, then the corresponding genus automatically applies as well, since the genus is simply a more general character. So if justice entails virtue, its opposite injustice entails vice, the opposite genus. If the analogy were apt, Parmenides' conclusion could be established. Since it has been shown that difference entails likeness, its opposite sameness entails unlikeness.

Aristotle should recognize that this analogy is false. It is false, because if two objects are different, Parmenides can argue both that they are unlike and that they are like on the basis of that difference. Since difference entails both unlikeness and likeness, it cannot be related to either of them as species to genus. So neither can its opposite, sameness. Indeed, if two objects are the same, they have to be like, not unlike, owing to that sameness. Parmenides could easily have shown that the one and the others are unlike, since they differ in many respects. Instead he takes the most implausible route available and makes the most plausible case he can for it.

Socrates counted likeness as a form at stage one of Parmenides' inquiry about the scope of forms in Part I (130b), and he would

---

137. On these items as opposites, cf. the *Sophist*, where Plato shows that we cannot solve the problem of not-being if we treat being and not-being as opposites (*enantia*) on a par with motion and rest, which exclude each other. See especially the puzzles about not-being at 239c–240c and 240c–241b, and Plato's solution at 257b–c. A similar error is exploited in the case of sameness and difference and likeness and unlikeness in the *Parmenides*, and presumably the puzzles are ripe for a similar solution.

presumably include unlikeness, sameness, and difference as forms at stage one as well. What are the implications of the present discussion for that assessment? Should Socrates reject such entities as forms? This seems not to be Plato's own conclusion, since he treats sameness and difference as great kinds in the *Sophist* and carefully analyzes their behavior. Maybe the moral of this discussion is that we too should investigate the unusual behavior of these relations.

Appendix to Deductions 1 and 2 (155e–157b)

As we have seen, Deductions 1 and 2 consider consequences for the one, starting from a positive hypothesis. Their conclusions conflict with each other. Deduction 1 examined what the one is solely in virtue of itself, apart from everything else, and showed that it is nothing at all, not even itself. Deduction 2 then examined what the one is in virtue of other things, with no priority to what it is in itself, and showed that it is everything indiscriminately. What should we make of the antinomy between Deductions 1 and 2? The Appendix and Deduction 3 offer different suggestions.

The Appendix attempts to reconcile the conclusions of Deductions 1 and 2 by supposing that the one is in those states at different times.[138] There is no contradiction if an object is F at one time and not-F at another.[139] Take a pair of opposites, say

---

138. For interpretations of the Appendix, see the symposium by Strang 1974 and Mills 1974, and Bostock 1978.

139. The Appendix is clearly relying on the Law of Non-Contradiction in its solution to the first antinomy. If the one partakes and does not partake of the same thing at the same time, it will violate the Law. Parmenides says:

"So it partakes at one time, and doesn't partake at another; for only in this way could it both partake and not partake of the same thing." (155e)

In discussing the Appendix, I continue to use the phrase "F and not-F" to specify a pair of opposites. But notice that sometimes, as in the passage just quoted, a more perspicuous phrase would be "is F and is-not F." We can go on using the original phrase if we recognize that being and not-being can themselves be values of "F" and "not-F."

motion and rest. If an object is in motion at one time and at rest at another, it must change from motion to rest. When does it change? If it is in motion, it has not yet changed. If it is at rest, it has already changed. When it changes must it not be neither in motion nor at rest? But there can be no time when a thing is neither in motion nor at rest (156c).[140] Parmenides proposes that the change between the two states occurs at an instant, and that the instant is not in time. At that instant the object is neither in motion nor at rest, but is poised for both alternatives (156d–e). Now extend the point about motion and rest to being and not-being (or to one and many). Whereas Deduction 1 argued that the one does not partake of being, Deduction 2 argued that it does. According to the Appendix, there is an instant at which the one changes from not-being to being, and at that instant it neither is nor is not (156e–157a).

This proposal is supposed to solve the first antinomy. Yet in saving the one from violating the Law of Non-Contradiction by proposing that it is F and not-F at different times, Parmenides allows the one to violate the Law of Excluded Middle at the instant. At the instant of change the one is neither F nor not-F. But logic demands that it be one or the other.

The One and the Others

Deductions 3 and 4 start from the positive hypothesis that one is, but they derive consequences for the others. Again their conclusions conflict with each other. Deduction 3 is the most constructive section in the whole of Part II. It integrates the approaches of Deductions 1 and 2 by considering both what the others are in virtue of themselves and what they are in virtue of the one. We also learn a great deal about what oneness contributes to other things. Parmenides argues that the others depend on oneness to be collective wholes, to be individual parts that compose those wholes, and to have determinate relations with one another. Deduction 4 then destroys what Deduction 3 has achieved by showing that the one cannot perform these functions

---

140. Parmenides also relies on the Law of Excluded Middle. At any given time an object must be either F or not-F.

and still be one. Deductions 3 and 4 constitute the second antinomy.

Deduction 3 (157b–159b)

If one is, what are the consequences for the others? Parmenides first points out that since they are others, the others are not the one—that is, they are non-identical with it (157b). Nonetheless, the others have some relation to the one. He says:

> "And yet the others are not absolutely deprived of the one, but somehow partake of it."—"In what way?"—"In that things other than the one are surely other because they have parts; for if they didn't have parts, they would be altogether one."—"That's right."— "And parts, we say, are parts of that which is a whole."—"Yes, we do."—"Yet the whole of which the parts are to be parts must be one thing composed of many, because each of the parts must be part, not of many, but of a whole." (157c)

This passage suggests that the others partake of the one by being wholes and are other than it by having parts. By implication, the one itself lacks parts, even though it is participated in. Otherwise the others would not be different from it. Whatever the manner of the participation, the one is "altogether one," and so is apparently not multiplied by instance-parts. Deduction 3 ignores the idea developed both in the Whole-Part Dilemma in Part I and in the second argument for unlimited multitude in Deduction 2 (143a–144e),[141] that the one itself is many by having many instance-parts. This consideration will be reintroduced in Deduction 4, with the disturbing outcome that nothing can partake of the one. Deduction 3 reaches positive results by overlooking the problem.

What does the one contribute to the others that makes them wholes? Parmenides says that a whole is one thing composed of many. What is the difference between a whole, which is composed of many parts, and a mere plurality of things? He attempts to clarify the difference by arguing that a part cannot be part of many. The argument is compressed and problematic:[142]

---

141. Discussed above, pp. 77–79.

142. I am grateful to Paul Coppock for his insight into this perplexing argument. I have also profited from reading Allen 1983, 267, and Harte 1994, 85–96.

"If something were to be part of many, in which it itself is, it will, of course, be both part of itself, which is impossible, and of each one of the others, if in fact it is part of all of them. For if it is not part of one, it will be part of the others, that one excepted, and thus it will not be part of each one. And if it is not part of each, it will be part of none of the many. But if something is part of none, it cannot be a part, or anything else at all, of all those things of which it is no part of any."—"It certainly appears so." (157c–d)

The argument appears to involve two fallacies: Parmenides assumes, first, that if something is part of all of a plurality, it is part of each member of that plurality; and second, that if something is not part of each member of a plurality, it is part of none of them (or not part of any of them). In the context, however, only the second is a fallacy.

Consider the first stage of the argument. This section looks fallacious, because we expect that if something is part of many, the many form a collection. To be part of a collective many is simply to be a member of the group. But this option is here excluded, because the argument turns on a distinction between a mere plurality (many) and a whole. If the many are not a whole, they cannot be viewed collectively—that is, all together or as a group. Instead they must be viewed distributively—or one by one.[143] If the many are regarded distributively, the first stage of the argument is valid. If something is part of many things, taken distributively, it has to be part of *each* of the many. Take the letter A, and suppose that it is part of all the words that begin with the letter A—"animal," "air," "atom," "apple," and so on. If the letter A is to be part of all words that begin with the letter A, it must be part of each of them. So it must also be part of the word "a." But, says Parmenides, it is impossible for something to be part of itself.[144] So something that is one of many cannot be a part of it. That is the conclusion he aimed to establish.

---

143. Cf. Allen 1983, 267; and Harte 1994, 90–91.

144. Parmenides is speaking only of proper parts: a thing is the same as itself, not part of itself. See 146b, where he lists four ways for A to be related to B and treats them as mutually exclusive and jointly exhaustive: A can be (1) the same as B, (2) different from B, (3) related to B as part to whole, or (4) related to B as whole to part. So if A is the same as B, it cannot be part of B.

He goes on, however, and the last part of the argument is fallacious. He now assumes that if something is not part of each of the many it is part of none of them (or not part of any of them). The many must still be regarded distributively, since they do not constitute a whole. If something fails to be part of each of the many, we cannot conclude that it is not part of any of them: it could be part of some of them. Think again of all words that begin with the letter A. Although the letter A is not part of each word in the totality (since it is not part of the word "a"), it is part of some of them (i.e., all the others). Perhaps this is a genuine mistake on Plato's part, since it occurs in the midst of an otherwise constructive discussion. Still, even here the conclusion has already been established before the fallacy is introduced. The point is that a member of a mere plurality cannot be a part of it, because to be a part of it, it would have to be part of each member. It cannot be a part of each member, because it is itself a member of the plurality, and nothing is part of itself.

A part, then, must be part of a whole. Thus Parmenides continues:

> "So the part would not be part of many things or all, but of some one character and of some one thing, which we call a 'whole,' since it has come to be one complete thing composed of all. This is what the part would be part of."—"Absolutely."—"So if the others have parts, they would also partake of some one whole."—"Certainly."— "So things other than the one must be one complete whole with parts."—"Necessarily." (157d–e)

At the outset Parmenides said that the others "somehow partake" of the one. He has argued that the others partake of the one by being wholes composed of parts. A whole is any complete thing that has parts. Included as wholes will presumably be not only physical objects with physical parts but also, and more important for the *Parmenides*, intelligible characters, like the form of human being, the form of justice, or any other unified complex character. This argument suggests that what the one contributes to the others is not an additional feature on a par with the determinate features they have. Instead, the one determines something about that entity's features, converting them into a whole that can be viewed all together.

In the next section we learn that the parts also partake of the one, but in their case the one accounts, not for the unity of something composed of parts, but rather for the individuality of something singular (157e–158a). According to Deduction 3, oneness functions in two fundamental ways. It accounts both for the unity of wholes and for the singularity of parts that compose those wholes.

Participation in the one does even more than this. The one not only determines items as individuals and binds them into wholes: we are told that the one also limits the parts in relation to each other and in relation to the whole, and the whole in relation to them. This suggests that the one accounts for the organization of parts in a unified whole.

In clarifying this point, Parmenides first considers what the others are apart from the one. He says that, stripped of oneness, things that partake of it—whether they partake of the oneness of parts or the oneness of wholes—are in themselves unlimited in multitude (158b–c). Here "unlimited in multitude" apparently means not merely that the others are a countless many (158b) but that they are an indeterminate many. It is by their communion with the one that both wholes and parts gain determination in relation to each other:

> "Furthermore, whenever each part comes to be one part, the parts then have a limit in relation to each other and in relation to the whole, and the whole has a limit in relation to the parts."—"Quite so."—"Accordingly, it follows for things other than the one that from the one and themselves gaining communion with each other, as it seems, something different comes to be in them, which affords a limit for them in relation to each other; but their own nature, by themselves, affords unlimitedness."—"Apparently."—"In this way, indeed, things other than the one, taken both as wholes and part by part, are both unlimited and partake of a limit."—"Certainly." (158c–d)

According to this passage, the others are unlimited in virtue of themselves. Through their communion with the one something different comes to be in them that limits them in relation to each other.[145] So communion with the one transforms an indetermi-

---

145. Cf. this passage with Aristotle, *Metaphysics* Z.17, 1041b11–33. Aristotle, too, uses the phrase *heteron ti* ("something different") in a discussion of parts and wholes. He uses the phrase to specify the form that

nate many into an organized whole, with parts determined as what they are in relation to each other and in relation to the whole, and the whole determined as what it is in relation to the parts. Parmenides is suggesting that the one is the *principle of structure* for the entities it combines.

Deduction 4 (159b–160b)

Deduction 4 undermines the conclusions of Deduction 3 by arguing that the others cannot partake of the one without fragmenting it into many. This deduction bears a closer resemblance than any other to arguments in Part I, with echoes of both the Whole-Part Dilemma and the Separation Argument. Here Parmenides argues that the one is separate from the others, and the others separate from it (159b–c). They are separate by existing apart from each other—that is, the one is not *in* them. Deduction 4 agrees with Deduction 3 that what is really one lacks parts. But whereas Deduction 3 allowed the others somehow to partake of the one even though it lacked parts, Deduction 4 excludes this participation. Since the one is separate from the others and lacks parts, it cannot be in them as a whole, nor can parts of it be in them. So, he says, the others can in no way partake of the one, if they partake neither by getting some part of it nor by getting it as a whole (159c–d).[146] Since participation in the one would multiply it, the one cannot perform the various functions attributed to it in Deduction 3.

We might think that young Aristotle should offer some resistance here. After all, in the fifth movement of the interrogation in Part I, Socrates proposed an alternative conception of participation to avoid the whole-part dilemma. If the one is a pattern and the others partake of it by being its likenesses, the one could exist apart from the others and lack parts, and nonetheless be participated in. However, the pattern-copy model of participation was eliminated in Part I, because it gave rise to an infinite regress. So if Aristotle were to reintroduce that option now, he would also have to rectify the misconception that gave rise to the regress. He is not yet in a position to do that. As we shall

---

organizes the parts, so that, e.g., the syllable "ab" differs from the syllable "ba," though they are both composed of the same parts.

146. Cf. Whole-Part Dilemma, esp. 131e.

see, Parmenides generates a similar regress in the next deduction
(162a–b). Not only does Aristotle not resist the argument in
Deduction 5, he applauds it with some of his most enthusiastic
responses. Until there is a solution to the Likeness Regress, or
until someone proposes another analysis of participation that
avoids Parmenides' objections, the only possibilities available are
those Parmenides himself proposed in the Whole-Part Dilemma,
distasteful as they were to Socrates.

If the one is separate from the others, and the others do not
partake of it, the one and the others not only exist apart, they
are also ontologically independent—as were forms and visible
things in the Separation Argument in Part I. So the others must
be determined as what they are without reference to the one.
According to the Separation Argument, things in our realm are
determined as what they are in relation to each other. Deduction
4 does not entertain that possibility.[147] Instead Parmenides argues
that the others have no features if they do not partake of the
one. He says that they are not one or many, nor are they like
or unlike the one (159e). They have no features, because to
partake of any character they would have to partake of one.[148]
Since they do not partake of one, they also do not partake of
more than one. So they partake of none.

Deduction 4 completes the investigation of the positive hypothesis, and it ends with the following statement:

> "Thus if one is, the one is all things and is not even one, both in
> relation to itself and, likewise, in relation to the others."—"Exactly."
> (160b)

The placement of this claim is striking. Why at the end of his
treatment of the positive hypothesis does Parmenides mention
the conclusions of only Deductions 1 and 2, ignoring the more
recent results of Deductions 3 and 4? Those who have read the

---

147. In reading 159d–160b, notice that Parmenides only considers what
the others are in relation to the one and concludes that they have no
features. Since he fails to consider what they are in relation to each
other, there may still be room for them to be somehow specified by
those relations, as in the Separation Argument in Part I. Parmenides
will reconsider that possibility in Deductions 7 and 8.

148. Notice that here "one" applies to any character.

whole of Part II know that Deduction 8, which completes the treatment of the negative hypothesis, ends with a summary of all eight deductions (166c). Reflecting on that statement, some scholars have thought that there should be a similar summary here, which mentions consequences both for the one and for the others.[149] But Parmenides does not give such a summary. Instead he simply states the contradiction between the conclusions of Deductions 1 and 2—something he could have done at the end of Deduction 2. This contradiction forces us to reject the positive hypothesis in favor of the negative hypothesis. Indeed, each side of the contradiction is sufficient to force the negative hypothesis. For it cannot be the case, if one is, that it is not even one (if it is not even one, it is nothing); nor can it be the case that it is everything (if it is everything, it is an impossible object with incompatible properties). The rejection of the positive hypothesis is overdetermined.

Did Parmenides save the statement until now simply because he had promised at the outset to discuss consequences for the others, as well as the one? In retrospect we might ask: What was the point of considering the one's contributions to the others in Deduction 3, if we already had sufficient reason to reject the positive hypothesis? Recall that the Appendix tried and failed to reconcile the conclusions of Deductions 1 and 2. Deduction 3 ignored that failure. In Deduction 3 Parmenides assumed that the one is altogether one and that the others can somehow partake of it. On that assumption he derived a number of constructive results. Deduction 4 then undermined those results by pointing out that the others cannot partake of the one without fragmenting it into many. Aren't these results now beside the point? The statement at the end of Deduction 4 tends to reinforce that impression, since it ignores them.

There may be another explanation for the presence of Deductions 3 and 4 and for their omission from a statement that prepares the way for the negative hypothesis. Perhaps these two

---

149. See Meinwald 1991, 142–44, who defends Heindorf's supplement of the Greek text at 160b3, which would result in just such a summary. If one adopts Heindorf's conjecture, the translation at 160b reads: "Thus if one is, the one is all things and is not even one, both in relation to itself and in relation to the others, and likewise the others."—"Exactly."

deductions give a clue to how the positive hypothesis might be saved. We shall return to this suggestion at the end of the introduction.

Since Parmenides has excluded the positive hypothesis, he now turns to the negative hypothesis. Deductions 5 and 6 examine consequences for the one, and Deductions 7 and 8 examine consequences for the others, starting from the hypothesis that one is not.

Being and Not-Being

As with the preceding antinomies, Deductions 5 and 6 derive conclusions that conflict with each other. Each derives consequences for the one, but those of Deduction 5 are positive, those of Deduction 6 negative. The focus of both deductions is being and not-being and the operation of negation: What do we mean when we say "one *is not*"?

Deduction 5 (160b–163b)

Deduction 5 appears to assume that by "one is not" we mean that the one partakes of not-being.[150] In Deduction 5 not-being is a character on a par with being, oneness, sameness, and the rest, and partaking of this character in no way deprives the one of other properties and relations. In the course of Deduction 5 we learn that the one is many things, even though it is not. Since we know what object we are talking about when we say "one is not," we do not confuse it with largeness, smallness, or anything else. We can therefore be assured, first, that our object is knowable, and second, that it is different from other things (160c). Parmenides goes on to demonstrate that the one is unlike the others, like itself, unequal to the others, and so on.

Then at 161e he makes a startling announcement:

"Furthermore, it [the one] must also somehow partake of being."—"How is that?"—"It must be in the state we describe; for if it is not so, we wouldn't speak truly when we say that the one is not. But

---

150. This assumption is analogous to the assumption in Deduction 2 (142b–c), where Parmenides took the hypothesis "if one is" to indicate that the one partakes of being.

if we do speak truly, it's clear that we say things that are. Isn't that so?"—"It is indeed so."—"And since we claim to speak truly, we must claim also to speak of things that are."—"Necessarily." (161e–162a)

Why does Parmenides think that the one, which has been hypothesized not to be, also partakes of being? He says:

> "Therefore, as it seems, the one *is* a not-being; for if it is not to *be* a not-being, but is somehow to give up its being in relation to not-being, it will straightway be a being."—"Absolutely." (162a)

Recall our earlier discussion of Plato's use of the verb "to be."[151] He uses the verb both as an incomplete predicate (as in "A is B") and as a complete predicate (as in "A is"). In this passage Parmenides uses "is" as an incomplete predicate which links the subject to a complement. The complement in this case is "a not-being." Just as "is" links the subject to the complement in the sentence "Socrates is a man," so it links the subject to the complement in the sentence "the one is a not-being." According to Parmenides, the one is a not-being because it partakes of being (a link) in relation to not-being. Were that link to be replaced by the link not-being, the one would *not-be* a not-being, and so would be a being instead. Not-being, too, can serve as a link between an object and a character. Whereas being links an object to a character it has, not-being links it to a character it lacks.

In the next section Parmenides calls being and not-being "bonds" to signify their role as links. Having already explained how something is a not-being, he extends the account to something that is a being. Whereas something is a not-being by partaking of being (bond) in regard to not-being, something is a being by partaking of not-being (bond) in regard to not-being. Something is a being by not being a not-being:

> "So if it is not to be, it must have *being* a not-being as a bond in regard to its not-being, just as, in like manner, what is must have *not-being* what is not, in order that it, in its turn, may completely be." (162a)

What should we make of Parmenides' claims? Take a sentence, for instance, "Largeness is one." What is the state of affairs

---

151. See above, pp. 69–71.

that makes that sentence true? According to Socrates' theory of participation in Part I, "Largeness is one" is true because largeness partakes of oneness. Parmenides' present proposal is that "Largeness is one" is true because largeness partakes of being in relation to (or in regard to) oneness.

This is not a new suggestion. Recall the end of Deduction 1, where Parmenides argued that the one is not even one. He got that result by claiming that for the one to be one it would have to partake of being. Since the one did not partake of being, it was deprived even of its own character. Parmenides said: "Therefore neither *is* it in such a way as to be one, because it would then, by being and partaking of being, be" (141e). In Deduction 1, as in Deduction 5, being is treated as a bond that connects an object to its character. Since Deduction 1 considered what the one is solely in virtue of its oneness, it turned out that the one could not even be one, because it would have to partake of being to bind it to its character.

In Deduction 5 Parmenides offers his proposal as the correct way to understand predication. Three items are specified in a sentence like "largeness is one": an object referred to by the subject expression "largeness," a bond specified by the copula "is," and a character specified by the predicate "one." Largeness partakes of being, which links it to oneness. What is the advantage of supposing that largeness partakes of being in relation to oneness over supposing that largeness partakes of oneness directly?

The advantage, if any, is far from plain. Parmenides has analyzed "x partakes of F" as "x partakes of being in relation to F." Thus he has analyzed the relation of participation as "partakes of being in relation to." If x is F by partaking of being in relation to F, what makes it the case that x is—or, as Parmenides would put the point in Deduction 5, that x is a being? Must x partake of being in relation to being? If being is a bond-character that links the subject to its own or some other character, must there be a further bond that links the subject to the bond-character? If so, a regress is in the offing.

In the next section of text, Parmenides claims to explicate how what is would completely be and how what is not would completely not be. Instead of simplifying the analysis, the explication complicates it. Notice that the analysis in each case now involves four entities rather than three. The subject is tied to the complement via two bonds rather than one:

> "This is how what is would most of all be and what is not would not be: on the one hand, by what is, if it is completely to be, partaking of being in regard to being a being and of not-being in regard to being a not-being; and, on the other hand, by what is not, if in its turn what is not is completely not to be, partaking of not-being in regard to not-being a not-being and of being in regard to being a not-being."—"Very true." (162a–b)[152]

Parmenides has offered two analyses for what is and two for what is not.[153] Let us set them out separately:

1a What is partakes of being in regard to being a being.
1b What is partakes of not-being in regard to being a not-being.
2a What is not partakes of not-being in regard to not-being a not-being.
2b What is not partakes of being in regard to being a not-being.

(1a) and (1b) are both supposed to be explications of "what is *is*," and both (2a) and (2b) are supposed to be explications of "what is not *is not*." To grasp how the explications work, we should recognize that if the subject partakes of being, then it has the next character in the series (and the link itself adds nothing); if the subject partakes of not-being, then it has the negation of the next character in the series. Two negatives yield a positive. (1a) says that what is:

1a* is a being.

(1b) says that what is:

1b* is not a not-being (i.e., is a being).

(2a) says that what is not:

2a* is not not a not-being (i.e., is a not-being).

---

152. This translation is based on the manuscript readings, not on the text as printed by Burnet in the Oxford edition. See note to the translation at 162b.

153. A different interpretation of this passage is given by Shorey 1891 and by Kahn 1981, 115–17 (who relies on the Shorey's textual changes printed by Burnet). An account of the Neoplatonic reading is given by Kohnke 1957.

(2b) says that what is not:

   2b* is a not-being.

Parmenides has touted this as a full analysis, but of course it is not. The subject is said to partake of the first bond. So a new bond is needed to connect the subject to that bond. And since the subject will partake of the new bond, there will have to be another bond, and so on indefinitely. An unlimited number of bonds are needed to connect an object to its character. Far from providing an explication, Parmenides has subverted the original analysis. He has revealed a Bradley-type regress similar to the one that I suggested was at work in the Likeness Regress in Part I.

What has gone wrong? Perhaps the mistake is to suppose that a bond is needed to link an object to its character. Or perhaps the mistake is to suppose that a bond between an object and its character is simply another character the subject partakes of. A bond is a relation between entities. Does Parmenides generate the regress by treating a relation as though it were a property?

We should think about Socrates' treatment of relations in Part I and Parmenides' treatment of them in Part II.[154] We think of properties as intrinsic to the objects to which they belong, and relations as holding between objects. Although relations are grounded in properties things have, they are themselves extrinsic to the objects. If I say "Simmias is like Socrates," likeness is a relation grounded in properties that Simmias and Socrates share. They are like because both are human beings, virtuous, and so on. Likeness is not a further property that Simmias and Socrates share. Now recall what Socrates said about likeness in his long speech. He said that two objects come to be like each other by getting a share of the form of likeness (129a). They have likeness because they partake of the form (130b, 130e–131a). Whatever an immanent character is—whether it is the whole of a form, is part of it, or simply corresponds to it—the immanent character is *in* the object that has it. So likeness is *in* Simmias. Likeness and other relations are treated as though they were properties on a par with redness or virtue.

---

154. A great deal has been written on Plato's treatment of relations. For one helpful discussion, see Matthen 1982.

When Parmenides speaks of relations in Part II, he also typically treats them as though they were properties. For instance, if he wants to say that A is unlike B, he says: "A partakes of (or has) unlikeness in relation to (*pros*) B."[155] Again, when he speaks of being as a bond between a subject and a character, he says: "A partakes of being in relation to B" (e.g., "the one partakes of being in relation to not-being"). Thus he treats unlikeness and other relations as though they were relational properties—properties an object has in relation to something.[156] The important point is that an object has a relational property only if it stands in a certain relation to something. We cannot do away with relations by treating them all as relational properties. Deduction 5 shows that if we treat all relations as though they were properties, an object must partake of an infinite number of properties to partake of any. The moral of this observation is that Socrates had better work out what a relation is before he posits a theory of forms.

Deduction 6 (163b–164b)

Scholars have sometimes asked whether Plato in the *Sophist* is interested in existence puzzles of the sort that have exercised twentieth-century philosophers. For instance, how can we coherently say "Pegasus does not exist"? We indicate something, Pegasus, and at the same time say that he is not there to be talked about.[157] As we have remarked, in the *Parmenides* (and also in the *Sophist*), Plato assumes that if x is F then x is.[158] Given this view, Plato has no problem about Pegasus. Pegasus is (= exists), since we can describe him. Many more things exist in Plato's ontology than exist in ours. For him anything describable is.

What, then, are we saying when we hypothesize that one *is not*? In Deduction 5 Parmenides interpreted the hypothesis to

---

155. See 161a; cf. 150d, 161b–c.

156. Cf. an example from the Separation Argument in Part I. Someone is a master in relation to someone who is a slave. Being a master is a relational property, a property an object has in virtue of standing in a certain relation to something (in this case the mastership relation).

157. On this topic, see N. P. White 1993, Introduction, and Kahn 1976.

158. See above, p. 71.

mean that the one partakes of not-being—a character on a par
with largeness, smallness, or any other character. So of course
the one was describable: it was different from other things, unlike
other things, like itself, and so on. The central puzzle of the
fifth deduction was that the one also partakes of being, which
connects it to its not-being (and to all its other characters). So
the one appeared to need unlimited shares of being simply to
be a not-being. Evidently that is not the way to understand "one
is not."

So Deduction 6 reconsiders what we mean when we say "one
is not." This time Parmenides proposes that by "is not" we mean
the absence of being for whatever we say is not (163c). He says:

> "When we say that something is not, are we saying that in a way
> it is not, but in a way it is? Or does this 'is not' signify without
> qualification that what is not is in no way at all and does not in
> any way partake of being?"—"Absolutely without qualification."—
> "Therefore what is not could neither be nor partake of being in any
> other way at all."—"No, it couldn't." (163c–d)

Since the one in no way partakes of being, it can partake of
no other character either. Parmenides says:

> "But in fact nothing that is belongs to it; for then, by partaking of
> that, it would partake of being."—"Clearly." (163e–164a)

The second part of the *Parmenides* has given two reasons why
an object that partakes of any character thereby partakes of being.
First, Deduction 2 claimed that being is distributed to everything
that is anything at all (144a–c).[159] Oneness is a being, all the
numbers are beings, largeness is a being, and so on. So if the
one partook of any character it would thereby partake of being.
Second, Deduction 5 claimed that being is a bond that ties an
object to any character it has. So if the one partook of any character, it would partake of being to tie it to that character. Accordingly, since the one in no way partakes of being, it can have no
character at all.

How can we talk about something that is nothing at all? The
sixth deduction is Plato's version of the modern-day puzzle about
Pegasus. We shouldn't even use the word "something" (164a),

---

159. See above, pp. 77–78.

as I did just now when I said "How can we talk about *something* that is nothing at all?" We shouldn't use words like "something," because there is nothing—no object—that we are talking about.[160] Because there is no object that we are talking about, Parmenides concludes Deduction 6 by saying that no knowledge, opinion, perception, account, name, or anything else is applicable to it (164b).

In Deduction 1 Parmenides reached the same conclusion, but starting from the positive hypothesis that the one is one. Having argued that the one was not even one (let alone anything else), and so nothing at all, he concluded that it had no name or account, and that there was no knowledge, perception, or opinion of it (142a). On that occasion he called into question the conclusion of his argument, and young Aristotle expressed his misgivings. Should we also have misgivings about the conclusion of Deduction 6? I suspect that we should, but for a different reason. In Deduction 1 Parmenides prompted us to have doubts, because Aristotle should never have agreed that the one is not (141e). Deduction 6, by contrast, starts from the negative hypothesis that the one is not, and Parmenides shows that if the one really is not, then it is nothing at all. The argument seems unimpeachable. To be sure, we can't legitimately talk about this indescribable object, since it is not there to be talked about. Still, we can compare Deduction 6 to Wittgenstein's ladder, which we must throw away once we have reached the top. If the one is not there to be talked about, then we should talk about other things.

Our misgivings should be of a different sort. If there is no oneness, what are the consequences for those other things? Parmenides turns to this question in Deductions 7 and 8.

Appearances

At first sight all appears to be well with the others, even though the one is not. But that is an illusion, as Parmenides will show.

---

160. Deduction 6 is worth comparing with the first three puzzles about not-being in the *Sophist* (237b–239c).

Deduction 7 (164b–165e)

Deduction 7 stands out against the background of stark abstractness that characterizes the other deductions. The effort required to make one's way through the previous deductions is rewarded by vivid imagery here. Deduction 7 is the counterpart of Deduction 3, deriving positive consequences for the others, but starting from the negative hypothesis about the one. If one is not, what follows for the others? The most striking feature of the seventh deduction is that nearly the whole of it is cast in terms of appearances. The others appear one and many, but aren't really so. They appear large, small, and equal, and they appear like and unlike themselves and each other, but they aren't really. Why is the argument about appearances?

Parmenides points out that if the others are other, they must be other than something. They can't be other than the one, if it is not, so they must be other than each other (164c).[161] Furthermore, they are other than each other as multitudes, because they cannot be so as ones, if one is not. He says of the others:

> "So they each are other than each other as multitudes; for they couldn't be so as ones, if one is not. But each mass of them, as it seems, is unlimited in multitude, and if you take what seems to be smallest, in an instant, just as in a dream, instead of seeming to be one, it appears many, and instead of very small, immense in relation to the bits chopped from it."—"That's quite right."—"The others would be other than each other as masses of this sort, if they are other, and if one is not."—"Quite so." (164c–d)

This passage suggests that there are a few things the others *are*: they are other than each other, and they are unlimited in multitude.

Beyond that is simply appearance. You take some small mass that seems to be one, but it suddenly disintegrates into many little bits. The small mass you started with now seems immense in relation to them. These are mere appearances, because without oneness to determine the individuality of things and the relations between them, the properties and relations we observe alter with our perspective. Later in the deduction Parmenides says:

---

161. Cf. Deduction 4 (159e–160b), which denied only that the others had features in relation to the one, and so left this possibility open.

> "So must not such a thing appear one to a person dimly observing from far off; but to a person considering it keenly from up close, must not each one appear unlimited in multitude, if in fact it is deprived of the one, if it is not?"—"Indeed, most necessarily."—"Thus the others must each appear unlimited and as having a limit, and one and many, if one is not, but things other than the one are."—"Yes, they must." (165b–c)

Imagine looking at a distant galaxy with the naked eye and then looking at it with a powerful telescope. At first you see one tiny glowing object, but then a multitude of stars. What you see depends on your perspective.

Notice that Parmenides says that the others appear, not only as having a limit, but as unlimited in multitude as well. This is a different claim from the earlier one that the others *are* unlimited in multitude. They are unlimited in multitude as masses lacking the determinateness the one could provide. They appear unlimited in multitude like a galaxy viewed through a telescope. Deduction 7 is reminiscent of the Separation Argument in Part I, suggesting that other things display lively diversity even though they fail to participate in the one. This appearance is deceptive, however, as Deduction 8 will now show.

Deduction 8 (165e–166c)

Deduction 8 is once again unadorned and abstract, but it is concise and to the point. If the one is not, but we suppose there are things other than the one, the others are neither one nor many. Nor do they even appear one or many. Nothing belongs to the others, nor is there even the appearance of anything belonging or not belonging to them. Without oneness, they cannot even be conceived as many, like or unlike, the same or different. Parmenides says:

> "The others neither are nor appear to be any of those things, if one is not."—"True."—"Then if we were to say, to sum up, 'if one is not, nothing is,' wouldn't we speak correctly?"—"Absolutely." (166b–c)

Deduction 8 undermines the conclusion of Deduction 7. The one not only determines boundaries between entities and structures them into integrated wholes; the one is also a precondition for the existence of items to be so organized. Without oneness to account for the singularity of parts, for the unity of wholes, and for the determinate relations between them, there is nothing at all—not even appearances.

The end of Deduction 8 sums up the results of all eight deductions:

> "Let us then say this [i.e., 'if one is not, nothing is'] – and also that, as it seems, whether one is or is not, it and the others both are and are not, and both appear and do not appear all things in all ways, both in relation to themselves and in relation to each other."— "Very true." (166c)

The Challenge

What should we make of this ending? The ending of Deduction 8 balances the conflicting conclusions of the four antinomies, thereby expressing multiple contradictions. Does this claim give us insight into, or even an inkling of, the truth?

Notice that Parmenides begins his final statement with a reminder of what Deduction 8 has shown ("Let us then say this [i.e., 'if one is not, nothing is']"), and that the summary itself is governed by the words "as it seems" (*hos eoiken*). Deduction 8 has *two* endings. The first is the real conclusion, which we will recognize if we speak "correctly" (*orthos*). The second is the apparent conclusion, which we will mistake for the real one if we have failed to see how Part II fits together into a coherent whole. If we have missed the point (as Plato perhaps expected), the conclusions of paired deductions will seem to carry equal weight, and the outcome will seem to be a collection of contradictions. But the first conclusion is the serious one. Deduction 8 has built on the preceding deductions to reach its verdict: if one is not, nothing is.

Let us review the steps that led to this devastating result. Deductions 1–4 considered the consequences, first for the one, then for the others, starting from the hypothesis that one is. Deduction 1 showed that if the one is considered in isolation from everything else, solely as what it is by itself, it is nothing at all. Deduction 2 showed that if the one is considered in its relations to everything else, with no priority to what it is in itself, it is everything indiscriminately. The Appendix tried to reconcile the results of the first antinomy by arguing that the one can be both F (where "F" stands for any conclusion in Deduction 2) and not-F (the opposite conclusion in Deduction 1) at different times. By proposing that the one is F and not-F at different times, the Appendix hoped to preserve all the foregoing conclusions and at the same time to guard against a violation of the Law of Non-Contradiction. Yet if the one is F and not-F at different times, it must change from F to not-F. Although Parmenides carefully insisted that there is no time at which an object can be neither F nor not-F, he allowed that at the instant of change (which is not in time) the one violates the Law of Excluded Middle. But it is impossible for something to be neither F nor not-F. The solution proposed in the Appendix will not work.

Recall the ending of Deduction 4, which concluded Parmenides' treatment of the positive hypothesis.[162] There Parmenides stated the contradiction between the conclusions of the first and second deductions. He could have made this statement at the end of Deduction 2. By the end of Deduction 2 there was already overwhelming reason to reject the positive hypothesis and to adopt the negative hypothesis instead. The contradiction between the conclusions of Deductions 1 and 2 forced the negative hypothesis, and each side of the contradiction forced it as well. The failure of the Appendix to save the positive hypothesis reinforced that outcome. Since Deductions 3 and 4 ignored the preceding results, and since the statement at the end of Deduction 4 ignored them, we too shall ignore Deductions 3 and 4 in our reconstruction of the overall argument.

We turn, then, to the negative hypothesis. Deductions 5 and 6 considered what we mean by the statement "one is not." Deduction 5 showed how not to understand it. If we assume that the one is not by partaking of being in relation to not-being, the one must have infinite shares of being even not to be. Deduction 6 then showed that if the one really is not, it is nothing at all. It is not there to be talked about.

Deductions 7 and 8 considered consequences for the others, on the hypothesis that one is not. By then we had taken a step beyond the situation described in the Separation Argument in Part I. In that argument there were stable objects; they simply failed to explain our world, and so were irrelevant to us. In

---

162. Above pp. 92–94.

Deductions 7 and 8 we assumed that there are no stable objects. According to Deduction 7 there is a lively and varied world even so—a world that exhibits a rich assortment of appearances. To be sure, there are no lasting objects, since the masses we catch sight of dissolve before our eyes; but there is a world nonetheless, with things appearing to have various properties through their interactions with one another. In Deduction 8 we learned that all this was an illusion. The masses we thought we saw aren't there after all. The one is required even for the masses to appear many and different from one another. Remove the one, and all things are indescribable. As Deduction 6 showed, what is indescribable is nothing at all. So if one is not, nothing is.

There is a lesson here. The lesson is that there must be forms, or stable objects of some sort, if there is to be any world at all. In the transitional section Parmenides said that there must be forms, if we are to have anywhere to turn our thought, and if we are to preserve the power of dialectic, a means of getting at the truth (135b–c). In Part II he showed that the consequences of denying the existence of forms are much more severe than we might have thought. At the end of Part I we were left with the impression that we might do without forms, though with a loss of precision. The insight we gain by going through the exercise in Part II is that there must be stable objects, and they must explain our world. We see this truth because we know that the conclusion of Deduction 8 is not true: There is a world to be explained.

How, then, did Parmenides arrive at the false conclusion in Deduction 8? Was there an error in the argument? Or did the conclusion rest on a false assumption? If we are persuaded by the overall sweep of the argument, we should suspect one or more of its assumptions. The most obvious assumption to question is the negative hypothesis itself, that one is not. Why not reject that hypothesis, since it yields an unacceptable outcome? We cannot simply reject it, since it was forced upon us. We were forced to accept it by the contradiction between the conclusions of Deductions 1 and 2, and also by each side of the contradiction. We had to adopt the negative hypothesis, given those conclusions.

So the question is this: Did those conclusions themselves rely on one or more false assumptions? Is there a way to save the

positive hypothesis by locating some false assumption that de-
stroyed it? It is now time to recall Deductions 3 and 4. Deductions
3 and 4 both considered consequences for the others, starting
from the hypothesis that one is. Deduction 3 produced some
highly constructive results by assuming that the one is altogether
one and that the others somehow partake of it. Deduction 4
overturned those conclusions by pointing out that if the one is
altogether one and in no way many, the others cannot partake
of it. If the others were to partake of the one, they would fragment
it into many, just as in the Whole-Part Dilemma in Part I.

Why assume, as Parmenides did in Deduction 4, that if the
one is one, it cannot be many? The only justification for this
assumption was Socrates' own commitment to it in his long
speech in Part I. This was the assumption that he challenged
Parmenides to refute (129d–130a). Instead of refuting it, Parmenides used it in Deduction 4 to undermine the constructive results
of Deduction 3. This assumption was also the source of the
trouble in Deductions 1 and 2. Deduction 1 showed that the one
is nothing at all by assuming that it is simply one and in no
way many. So the one cannot even *be* one without being many.
Deduction 2 showed that the one is everything by assuming that
the one is many and that its oneness is merely one of its many
properties. The extreme conclusions of Deductions 1 and 2 relied
on the same assumption, that the one cannot be both one and
many. Deduction 1 assumed that the one is simply one, and
Deduction 2 assumed that it is simply many.

The key issue in the second part of the *Parmenides* is Socrates'
assumption in Part I that the one cannot be both one and many.
This is the false assumption that ultimately leads to the conclusion in Deduction 8—and that conclusion is Parmenides' final
response to Socrates' original challenge in Part I. Socrates' assumption is false, and it must be false because there is a world
to be explained.

Our question is how to make sense of the idea that the one
is both one and many. How can the one be one, even though
other things partake of it, and it partakes of other things? This
question is the main challenge posed by the *Parmenides*. The
second part of the dialogue offers many clues to the answer,
and the first place to look for them is in Deduction 3. Although
this deduction focuses on consequences for the others, and so

does not answer our question directly, it offers a strategy that may help in answering it. Deduction 3 integrates the perspectives of Deductions 1 and 2. Instead of supposing that an object must be considered either as what it is in virtue of itself (the perspective of Deduction 1) or as what it is in virtue of other things (the perspective of Deduction 2), Deduction 3 considers what the others are both in virtue of themselves and in virtue of the one. This strategy can also be applied to the one.

But working out what the one is in virtue of itself and what it is in virtue of other things is not all that is required in answering our question. How can the one *be* one simply in virtue of itself? Must the one partake of being even to be itself? This is the problem posed by the first deduction, and Parmenides exploits it in Deduction 5. In Deduction 5 he argues that an object must partake of infinite shares of being to be anything at all, including itself. This problem about being is one version of the problem of participation, which is a central topic in Part I. More generally it is a problem about relations, since participation is a relation between an object and some character it has.

How shall we explain participation? Can we explicate participation in terms of being? Deduction 5 reveals the difficulties of such an analysis. If the being that binds an object to its character is just another character the object partakes of, then the object must partake of a further share of being to bind it to the first. To avoid this difficulty, we must either find another way to explicate participation or find a better way to understand the function of being as a bond.

Suppose we take the first route. Part I offers a number of alternative conceptions of participation. All are problematic, but perhaps they are correctable. For instance, perhaps the *Timaeus* offers a version of the pattern-copy model of participation that is immune to the objections in the first part of the *Parmenides*.

Or suppose we take the second route. Part II indicates repeatedly that the abstract objects whose behavior it explores function very differently from items like human being and animal, or redness and color, which are entities with determinate content. How do those abstract objects behave, and can we learn something from their behavior for the analysis of being? Think about the puzzle about likeness and unlikeness in Deduction 2 and the constructive investigation of the one and the others in

Deduction 3. These discussions suggest that the abstract entities discussed in Part II apply to objects on the basis of other, ultimately determinate properties the objects have, and do not contribute additional content themselves. Recall that in Deduction 3 the one is responsible for an object's singularity, for the collective unity of its parts, and for the determinate relations between those parts. Consider whether being might function similarly in connecting an object to its various features. And consider whether being contributes the same or a different structure in binding an object to itself (expressed in a statement of identity), to its proper character (expressed in a self-predication), and to characters other than its own (expressed in an ordinary predication).

The challenge is to show not only how the one can be both one and many, but also how it can *be* anything at all. Once you have worked out your own answers to these questions using the hints that Plato provides, apply them to the puzzles in Part I and see if you can save Socrates from his difficulties. That is the exercise. After that read the *Sophist*, the *Timaeus*, and the *Philebus*, and see how your proposals compare with Plato's own!

Bibliography

Ackrill, J. L. 1957. "Plato and the Copula: *Sophist* 251–259." *Journal of Hellenic Studies* 77. Repr. in Allen (ed.) 1965, 207–18; and in Vlastos (ed.) 1971, 210–22.

Allen, R. E. (ed.) 1965. *Studies in Plato's Metaphysics*. London.

———— 1970. "The Generation of Numbers in Plato's *Parmenides*." *Classical Philology* 65, 30–34.

———— 1974. "Unity and Infinity: *Parmenides* 142b–145a." *Review of Metaphysics* 27, 697–725.

———— 1983. *Plato's Parmenides*. Minneapolis.

Anscombe, G.E.M. 1966. "The New Theory of Forms." *The Monist* 50, 403–20. Repr. in G.E.M. Anscombe, *From Parmenides to Wittgenstein*. Minneapolis, 1981. 21–33.

Aristotle. Revised Oxford Translation. 2 vols. Ed. by J. Barnes. Princeton, 1984.

Aristoxenus. *Elementa Harmonica*. Ed. and trans. (into Italian) by Rosetta da Rios. Rome, 1954.

Bestor, T. W. 1978. "Common Properties and Eponymy in Plato." *Philosophical Quarterly* 28, 189–207.

———— 1980. "Plato's Semantics and Plato's *Parmenides*." *Phronesis* 25, 38–75.

Bostock, D. 1978. "Plato on Change and Time in the *Parmenides*." *Phronesis* 23, 229–42.

Bradley, F. H. 1897. *Appearance and Reality*. Second Edition. Oxford.

Brown, L. 1986. "Being in the *Sophist*: A Syntactical Inquiry." *Oxford Studies in Ancient Philosophy* 4, 49–70.

Brumbaugh, R. S. 1961. *Plato on the One*. New Haven.

Burnet, J. 1914. *Greek Philosophy*. Part 1: *Thales to Plato*. London.

Burnyeat, M. F. 1982. "Idealism and Greek Philosophy: What Descartes Saw and Berkeley Missed." *Philosophical Review* 91, 3–40.

———— 1990. *The Theaetetus of Plato*. Indianapolis.

Cherniss, H. 1932. "Parmenides and the *Parmenides* of Plato." *American Journal of Philology* 53, 122–38.

——— 1957. "The Relation of the *Timaeus* to Plato's Later Dialogues." *American Journal of Philology* 78. Repr. in Allen (ed.) 1965, 339–78.

Code, A. 1982. "On the Origins of Some Aristotelian Theses about Predication." In J. Bogen and J. E. McGuire (eds.), *How Things Are*. Dordrecht. 101–31.

Cohen, S. M. 1971. "The Logic of the Third Man." *Philosophical Review* 80, 448–75.

Cornford, F. M. 1939. *Plato and Parmenides*. London.

Crombie, I. M. 1963. *An Examination of Plato's Doctrines*. Vol. 2. London.

Curd, P. K. 1988. "Parmenidean Clues in the Search for the Sophist." *History of Philosophy Quarterly* 5, 307–20.

——— 1989. "Some Problems of Unity in the First Hypothesis of the *Parmenides*." *Southern Journal of Philosophy* 27, 347–59.

——— 1990. "*Parmenides* 142b5–144e7: The 'Unity Is Many' Arguments." *Southern Journal of Philosophy* 28, 19–35.

——— 1991. "Parmenidean Monism." *Phronesis* 36, 241–64.

Denyer, N. 1983. "Plato's Theory of Stuffs." *Philosophy* 58, 315–27.

Descartes, R. *Meditations*. Trans. by D. Cress. Indianapolis, 1979.

Diels, H., and W. Kranz 1951. *Die Fragmente der Vorsokratiker*. 3 vols. Zürich.

Diès, A. 1923. *Platon Parménide*. Paris.

Dodds, E. R. 1928. "The *Parmenides* of Plato and the Origin of the Neoplatonic 'One'." *Classical Quarterly* 22, 129–42.

Fine, G. 1980. "The One over Many." *Philosophical Review* 89, 197–240.

——— 1984. "Separation." *Oxford Studies in Ancient Philosophy* 2, 31–87.

——— 1986. "Immanence." *Oxford Studies in Ancient Philosophy* 4, 71–97.

——— 1993. *On Ideas*. Oxford.

Forrester, J. W. 1972. "Plato's *Parmenides*: The Structure of the First Hypothesis." *Journal of the History of Philosophy* 10, 1–14.

——— 1974. "Arguments an Able Man Could Refute: *Parmenides* 133b–134e." *Phronesis* 19, 233–37.

Frede, M. 1967. *Prädikation und Existenzaussage*. Göttingen.

——— 1992. "Plato's *Sophist* on False Statements." In R. Kraut (ed.), *The Cambridge Companion to Plato*. Cambridge. 397–424.

Freeman, K. 1948. *Ancilla to the Pre-Socratic Philosophers*. Cambridge, Mass.

Fujisawa, N. 1974. "Ἔχειν, Μετέχειν, and Idioms of 'Paradeigmatism' in Plato's Theory of Forms." *Phronesis* 19, 30–58.

Furley, D. J. 1992. "From Anaxagoras to Socrates." In K. J. Boudouris (ed.), *The Philosophy of Socrates*. Vol. 2. Athens. 74–80.

Gallop, D. 1975. *Plato: Phaedo*. Oxford.

Geach, P. T. 1956. "The Third Man Again." *Philosophical Review* 65. Repr. in Allen (ed.) 1965, 265–77.

Hardie, W.F.R. 1936. *A Study in Plato*. Oxford.

Harte, V. 1994. *Parts and Wholes: Plato, Aristotle, and the Metaphysics of Structure*. Dissertation, Cambridge University.

Hathaway, R. F. 1973. "The Second 'Third Man'." In Moravcsik (ed.) 1973, 78–100.

Jordan, R. W. 1983. *Plato's Arguments for Forms*. Cambridge.

Kahn, C. H. 1966. "The Greek Verb 'To Be' and the Concept of Being." *Foundations of Language* 2, 245–65.

—— 1976. "Why Existence Does Not Emerge as a Distinct Concept in Greek Philosophy." *Archiv für Geschichte der Philosophie* 58, 323–34.

—— 1981. "Some Philosophical Uses of 'To Be' in Plato." *Phronesis* 26, 105–34.

—— 1986. "Retrospect on the Verb 'To Be' and the Concept of Being." In S. Knuuttila and J. Hintikka (eds.), *The Logic of Being*. Dordrecht. 1–28.

Keyt, D. 1971. "The Mad Craftsman in the *Timaeus*." *Philosophical Review* 80, 230–35.

Kirchner, J. 1901–1903. *Prosographia Attica*. 2 vols. Berlin.

Kirk, G. S., J. E. Raven, and M. Schofield 1983. *The Presocratic Philosophers*. Second Edition. Cambridge.

Kohnke, F. W. 1957. "Plato's Conception of τὸ οὐκ ὄντως οὐκ ὄν." *Phronesis* 2, 32–40.

Lee, E. N. 1973. "The Second 'Third Man': An Interpretation." In Moravcsik (ed.) 1973, 101–22.

Lewis, F. A. 1979. "Parmenides on Separation and the Knowability of the Forms: Plato *Parmenides* 133a ff." *Philosophical Studies* 35, 105–27.

Lloyd, G.E.R. (ed.) 1978. *Hippocratic Writings*. Harmondsworth.

Lynch, W. F. 1959. *An Approach to the Metaphysics of Plato through the Parmenides*. Washington.

McCabe, M. M. 1994. *Plato's Individuals*. Princeton.

McKirahan, R. 1994. *Philosophy Before Socrates*. Indianapolis.

McPherran, M. L. 1983. "Plato's *Parmenides* Theory of Relations." In F. J. Pelletier and J. King-Farlow (eds.), *New Essays on Plato*. Guelph, Ont. 149–64.

Malcolm, J. 1991. *Plato on the Self-Predication of Forms*. Oxford.

Mates, B. 1979. "Identity and Predication in Plato." *Phronesis* 24, 211–29. Repr. in S. Knuuttila and J. Hintikka (eds.), *The Logic of Being*. Dordrecht, 1986.

Matthen, M. 1982. "Plato's Treatment of Relational Statements in the *Phaedo*." *Phronesis* 27, 90–100.

Meinwald, C. 1991. *Plato's Parmenides*. Oxford.

—— 1992. "Good-bye to the Third Man." In R. Kraut (ed.), *The Cambridge Companion to Plato*. Cambridge. 365–96.

Miller, M. H., Jr. 1986. *Plato's Parmenides: The Conversion of the Soul*. University Park, Pa.

Mills, K. W. 1974. "Plato and the Instant." *Proceedings of the Aristotelian Society* 48, 81–96.

Moline, J. 1981. *Plato's Theory of Understanding*. Madison.

Moravcsik, J. M. E. 1963. "The 'Third Man' Argument and Plato's Theory of Forms." *Phronesis* 8, 50–62.

—— (ed.) 1973. *Patterns in Plato's Thought*. Dordrecht.

—— 1982. "Forms and Dialectic in the Second Half of the *Parmenides*." In M. Schofield and M. Nussbaum (eds.), *Language and Logos*. Cambridge. 135–53.

Mourelatos, A.P.D. 1970. *The Route of Parmenides*. New Haven.

Nehamas, A. 1973. "Predication and Forms of Opposites in the *Phaedo*." *Review of Metaphysics* 26, 461–91.

—— 1979. "Self-Predication and Plato's Theory of Forms." *American Philosophical Quarterly* 16, 93–103.

Owen, G.E.L. 1953. "The Place of the *Timaeus* in Plato's Dialogues." *Classical Quarterly* N.S. 3. Repr. in Allen (ed.) 1965, 313–38; and in Owen 1986.

—— 1965. "The Platonism of Aristotle." *Proceedings of the British*

Academy 50, 125–50. Repr. in J. Barnes, M. Schofield, and R. Sorabji (eds.), *Articles on Aristotle*. Vol. 1. London, 1975; and in Owen 1986.

———— 1966. "Plato and Parmenides on the Timeless Present." *The Monist* 50, 317–40. Repr. in A.P.D. Mourelatos (ed.), *The Pre-Socratics*. Garden City, N.Y., 1974; and in Owen 1986.

———— 1968. "Dialectic and Eristic in the Treatment of the Forms." In Owen (ed.), *Aristotle on Dialectic: The Topics*. Oxford. 103–25. Repr. in Owen 1986.

———— 1970. "Notes on Ryle's Plato." In O. P. Wood and G. Pitcher (eds.), *Ryle*. New York. 341–72. Repr. in Owen 1986.

———— 1971. "Plato on Not-Being." In Vlastos (ed.) 1971, 223–67. Repr. in Owen 1986.

———— 1986. *Logic, Science and Dialectic*. Ithaca and London.

Page, D. L. 1962. *Poetae Melici Graeci*. Oxford.

Panagiotou, S. 1987. "The Day and Sail Analogies in Plato's *Parmenides*." *Phoenix* 41, 10–24.

Patterson, R. 1985. *Image and Reality in Plato's Metaphysics*. Indianapolis.

Peterson, S. 1973. "A Reasonable Self-Predication Premise for the Third Man Argument." *Philosophical Review* 82, 451–70.

———— 1981. "The Greatest Difficulty for Plato's Theory of Forms: The Unknowability Argument of *Parmenides* 133c–134c." *Archiv für Geschichte der Philosophie* 63, 1–16.

Plato. *Collected Dialogues*. Ed. by E. Hamilton and H. Cairns. Princeton, 1961.

———— *Opera*. 5 vols. Ed. by J. Burnet. Oxford, 1900–1907.

Prior, W. J. 1979. "*Parmenides* 132c–133a and the Development of Plato's Thought." *Phronesis* 24, 230–40.

———— 1983. "*Timaeus* 48e–52d and the Third Man Argument." In F. J. Pelletier and J. King-Farlow (eds.), *New Essays on Plato*. Guelph, Ont. 123–47.

———— 1985. *Unity and Development in Plato's Metaphysics*. London.

Proclus. *Commentary on Plato's Parmenides*. Trans. by G. R. Morrow and J. M. Dillon, with introduction and notes by J. M. Dillon. Princeton, 1987.

Robinson, R. 1953. *Plato's Earlier Dialectic*. Second Edition. Oxford.

Ross, W. D. 1953. *Plato's Theory of Ideas*. Second Edition. Oxford.

Runciman, W. G. 1959. "Plato's *Parmenides*." *Harvard Studies in Classical Philology* 64. Repr. in Allen (ed.) 1965, 149–84.

Russell, B. 1937. *The Principles of Mathematics*. Second Edition. Cambridge.

Ryle, G. 1939. "Plato's *Parmenides*." *Mind* 48. Repr. with afterword in Allen (ed.) 1965, 97–147.

Sayre, K. M. 1978. "Plato's *Parmenides*: Why the Eight Hypotheses Are Not Contradictory." *Phronesis* 23, 133–50.

———— 1983. *Plato's Late Ontology: A Riddle Resolved*. Princeton.

Scaltsas, T. 1992. "A Necessary Falsehood in the Third Man Argument." *Phronesis* 37, 216–32.

Schofield, M. 1973. "A Neglected Regress Argument in the *Parmenides*." *Classical Quarterly* N.S. 23, 29–44.

———— 1974. "Plato on Unity and Sameness." *Classical Quarterly* N.S. 24, 33–45.

———— 1977. "The Antinomies of Plato's *Parmenides*." *Classical Quarterly* N.S. 27, 139–58.

———— 1996. "Likeness and Likenesses in the *Parmenides*." In C. Gill and M. M. McCabe (eds.), *Form and Argument: Studies in Late Plato*.

Sellars, W. 1955. "Vlastos and 'The Third Man'." *Philosophical Review* 64, 405–37. Repr. in Sellars, *Philosophical Perspectives*. Reseda, Calif., 1967.

Shorey, P. 1891. "On *Parmenides* 162 A.B." *American Journal of Philology* 12, 349–53.

Smith, J. A. 1917. "General Relative Clauses in Greek." *Classical Review* 31, 69–71.

Spellman, L. 1983. "Patterns and Copies: The Second Version of the Third Man." *Pacific Philosophical Quarterly* 64, 165–75.

Strang, C. 1963. "Plato and the Third Man." *Proceedings of the Aristotelian Society* 37. Repr. in Vlastos (ed.) 1971, 184–200.

———— 1974. "Plato and the Instant." *Proceedings of the Aristotelian Society* 48, 63–79.

Taylor, A. E. 1934. *The Parmenides of Plato*. Oxford.

Teloh, H. 1976. "Parmenides and Plato's *Parmenides* 131a–132c." *Journal of the History of Ideas* 14, 125–30.

———— 1981. *The Development of Plato's Metaphysics*. University Park, Pa.

Thucydides. *History of the Peloponnesian War*. Trans. by R. Warner. Harmondsworth, 1954.

Vlastos, G. 1954. "The Third Man Argument in Plato's *Parmenides.*" *Philosophical Review* 63. Repr. with addendum in Allen (ed.) 1965, 231–63.

———— 1969. "Plato's 'Third-Man' Argument (*Parm.* 132a1–b2): Text and Logic." *Philosophical Quarterly* 19, 289–301. Repr. in Vlastos 1973.

———— (ed.) 1971. *Plato: A Collection of Critical Essays*. Vol. 1: *Metaphysics and Epistemology*. Garden City, N.Y.

———— 1973. *Platonic Studies*. Princeton.

Waterlow, S. 1982. "The Third Man's Contribution to Plato's Paradigmatism." *Mind* 91, 339–57.

Wedin, M. V. 1977. "αὐτὰ τὰ ἴσα and the Argument at *Phaedo* 74b7–c5." *Phronesis* 22, 191–205.

White, F. C. 1977. "Plato's Middle Dialogues and the Independence of Particulars." *Philosophical Quarterly* 27, 193–213.

White, N. P. 1993. *Plato: Sophist*. Indianapolis.

Wundt, M. 1935. *Platons Parmenides*. Stuttgart and Berlin.

Analysis of the
Deductions in Part II

Deduction 1 (137c–142a): If the one is one, what are the consequences for the one? Negative consequences.

Hypothesis D.1: If it is one (137c),
1. The one is not many (137c).
2. The one is not a whole and doesn't have parts (137c–d).
3. The one doesn't have a beginning, middle, or end (137d).
4. The one is unlimited (137d).
5. The one is without shape (137d–138a).
6. The one has no location (138a–b).
    A. The one is not in another (138a).
    B. The one is not in itself (138a–b).
7. The one is not in motion or at rest (138b–139b).
    A. The one is not in motion (138b–139a).
        (1) The one is not altered (138c).
        (2) The one does not move spatially (138c–139a).
            a. The one doesn't spin in the same location (138c–d).
            b. The one doesn't change place (138d–139a).
    B. The one is not at rest (139a–b).
8. The one is not the same as or different from another or itself (139b–e).
    A. The one is not different from itself (139b).
    B. The one is not the same as another (139b–c).
    C. The one is not different from another (139c).
    D. The one is not the same as itself (139d–e).
9. The one is not like or unlike another or itself (139e–140b).
    A. The one is not like another or itself (139e–140a).
    B. The one is not unlike another or itself (140a–b).
10. The one is not equal or unequal to another or itself (140b–d).
11. The one is not older or younger than, or the same age as, itself or another (140e–141a).
    A. The one is not the same age as another or itself (140e).

   B. The one is not older or younger than another or itself
       (140e–141a).
12. The one is not in time (141a–d).
13. The one is not (141d–e).
14. The one is not one (141e).
15. The one is not named or spoken of, and is not the object of
    opinion, knowledge, or perception (142a).

Deduction 2 (142b–155e): If one is, what are the consequences
for the one? Positive consequences.

Hypothesis D.2: If one is (142b),
   1. The one partakes of being (142b).
   2. Being is different from oneness (142b–c).
   3. The one is a whole and has parts (142c–d).
   4. The one is unlimited in multitude (142d–144e).
      Argument 1 (142d–143a).
      Argument 2 (143a–144e).
   5. The one is limited (144e–145a).
   6. The one has a beginning, middle, and end (145a–b).
   7. The one has a shape (145b).
   8. The one has a location (145b–e).
      A. The one is in itself (145b–c).
      B. The one is in a different thing (145c–e).
   9. The one is in motion and at rest (145e–146a).
      A. The one is at rest (145e–146a).
      B. The one is in motion (146a).
10. The one is the same as and different from the others and
    itself (146a–147b).
      A. The one is the same as itself (146b–c).
      B. The one is different from itself (146c–d).
      C. The one is different from the others (146d).
      D. The one is the same as the others (146d–147b).
11. The one is like and unlike the others and itself (147c–148d).
      A. The one is like the others (147c–148a).
      B. The one is unlike the others (148a–c).
      Second arguments for (A) and (B) (148c–d).
      C. The one is like itself (148d).
      D. The one is unlike itself (148d).
12. The one touches and does not touch the others and itself
    (148d–149d).

A. The one touches the others (148d–e).
B. The one touches itself (148d–e).
C. The one does not touch itself (148e–149a).
D. The one does not touch the others (149a–d).
13. The one is equal and unequal to the others and itself (149d–151b).
    A. The one is equal to the others (149d–150d).
    B. The one is equal to itself (150e).
    C. The one is greater and less than (i.e., unequal to) itself (150e–151a).
    D. The one is greater and less than (i.e., unequal to) the others (151a–b).
Corollary to 13: The one is of measures (and parts) equal to, and more and fewer than, itself and the others (151b–e).
14. The one partakes of time (151e–152a).
15. The one is and comes to be older and younger than itself and the others and neither comes to be older or younger than itself and the others (151e–155c).
    A. The one comes to be older and younger than itself (152a–b).
    B. The one is older and younger than itself (152b–d).
    C. The one is and comes to be the same age as itself (152e).
    D. The one is older than the others (152e–153b).
    E. The one is younger than the others (153b–d).
    F. The one is neither older nor younger than (i.e., is the same age as) the others (153d–154a).
    G. The one doesn't come to be older or younger than the others (154b–c).
    H. The one comes to be younger than the others (154c–155b).
    I. The others come to be younger than the one (155b).
16. The one partakes of time past, present, and future (155d).
17. The one is named and spoken of, and is the object of opinion, knowledge, and perception (155d–e).

Appendix to Deductions 1 and 2 (155e–157b): If the one is as described in Deductions 1 and 2, and it is in time, what are the consequences for it?

Hypothesis Appendix: If the one is both one and many (D.2) and neither one nor many (D.1), and it is in time (D.2) (155e),

1. The one partakes of being (one and many) at one time and doesn't partake at another, since this is the only way it could both partake and not partake of the same thing (155e).
2. There is a definite time when it gets a share of being and when it parts from it (156a).
3. The one comes to be and ceases to be when it gets and releases being (156a).
4. Take any state of motion (e.g., coming-to-be or ceasing-to-be) and subsequent state of rest (e.g., being or not-being) (156b): if an object is in a state of motion at one time and in a state of rest at another, it must change from one state to the other (156c).
5. When an object changes from motion to rest, it is neither in motion nor at rest (156c).
6. There is no time when an object can be neither in motion nor at rest (156c).
7. The change occurs at an instant, which is not in time (156d–e).
8. At the instant of change the one is neither in motion nor at rest (156e).
9. At the instant of change the one neither is nor is not, and neither comes to be nor ceases to be (157a).
10. Similarly with other opposed states and processes (157a–b).

Deduction 3 (157b–159b): If one is, what are the consequences for the others? Positive consequences.

Hypothesis D.3: If one is (157b),
1. The others are not the one (157b).
2. The others somehow partake of the one (157c).
   A. The others partake of the one as wholes (157c–e).
   B. The others partake of the one as parts (157e–158a).
3. The others are many (158b).
4. The others are unlimited and partake of a limit (158b–d).
   A. Things that get a share of the one are in themselves unlimited in multitude (158b–c).
   B. By partaking of the one, the others partake of a limit (158c–d).
5. The others are both like and unlike each other and themselves (158e–159a).
   A. The others are like each other and themselves (two arguments) (158e).

   B. The others are unlike themselves and each other (158e–159a).
  6. The others have all the opposite properties (159a–b).

Deduction 4 (159b–160b): If one is, what are the consequences for the others? Negative consequences.

Hypothesis D.4: If one is (159b),
1. The one is separate from the others, and the others are separate from the one (159b–c).
2. The others are in no way one (159c–d).
3. The others are not many (159d–e).
4. The others aren't like or unlike the one (159e–160a).
5. The others have no other properties (160a).

Conclusion of Deductions 1–4: The one is all things and is not even one, both in relation to itself and in relation to the others (160b).

Deduction 5 (160b–163b): If one is not, what are the consequences for the one? Positive consequences.

Hypothesis D.5: If one is not (160b),
1. The one is knowable (160b–c).
2. The one is different from the others, and they are different from it (160c–e).
3. The one partakes of *that, something, this, to this, these,* etc. (160e–161a).
4. The one is like and unlike (161a–c).
   A. The one is unlike the others, and they are unlike it (161a–b).
   B. The one is like itself (161b–c).
5. The one is unequal and equal (161c–e).
   A. The one is unequal to the others, and they are unequal to it (161c–d).
   B. The one is equal (161d–e).
6. The one somehow partakes of being (161e–162b).
7. The one has being and not-being (162b).
8. The one is both in motion and at rest (162b–e).
   A. The one is in motion (162b–c).
   B. The one is at rest (162c–e).
9. The one is both altered and not altered (162e–163a).

10. The one both comes to be and ceases to be and does not come to be or cease to be (163a–b).

Deduction 6 (163b–164b): If one is not, what are the consequences for the one? Negative consequences.

Hypothesis D.6: If one is not (163c),
  1. The one in no way partakes of being (163c–d).
  2. The one neither comes to be nor ceases to be (163d).
  3. The one is not altered (163d–e).
  4. The one is neither in motion nor at rest (163e).
  5. Nothing that is belongs to the one (163e–164a).
  6. The others are not related to it (164a).
     A. The others are neither like nor unlike it (164a).
     B. The others are neither the same as nor different from it (164a).
  7. Terms like *of that*, *to that*, *something*, *this*, etc., are not applicable to what is not (164a).
  8. Time past, hereafter, and now are not applicable to what is not (164b).
  9. Knowledge, opinion, perception, an account, a name, etc., are not applicable to what is not (164b).
  10. The one is in no state at all (164b).

Deduction 7 (164b–165e): If one is not, what are the consequences for the others? Positive consequences.

Hypothesis D.7: If one is not (164b),
  1. The others are other than each other (164b–c).
  2. The others are masses unlimited in multitude (164c–d).
  3. The others appear one, but aren't really so (164d).
  4. There seem to be a number of others, and some appear even and some odd, but they aren't really so (164d–e).
  5. The others appear unequal and equal (164e–165a).
  6. The others appear limited and unlimited (165a–c).
     Argument 1 (165a–b)
     A. A mass appears to have a limit in relation to another mass (165a).
     B. A mass appears to have no beginning, limit, or middle in relation to itself (165a–b).
     Argument 2 (165b–c)

   A. A mass appears one from far off (165b–c).
   B. A mass appears unlimited in multitude from up close
      (165c).
 7. The others seem to be both like and unlike themselves and
    each other (165c–d).
 8. The many appear to have all the other opposites (165d).

Deduction 8 (165e–166c): If one is not (but things other than the
   one are), what are the consequences for the others? Negative
   consequences.

Hypothesis D.8: If one is not (165e),
   1. The others are neither one nor many (165e).
   2. The others don't appear one or many (165e–166b).
   3. The others neither are nor appear to be anything at all (166b).
   4. Nothing is (166c).
Summary of Deductions 1–8 (166c).

PARMENIDES

Cephalus

When we arrived in Athens from home in Clazomenae, we ran 126
into Adeimantus and Glaucon in the marketplace. Adeimantus
took me by the hand and said, "Welcome, Cephalus. If there is
anything you want here that we can do for you, please tell us."[1]

"In fact that's the very reason I'm here," I replied, "to ask a
favor of you."

"Tell us what you want," he said.

And I replied, "Your half brother on your mother's side –   b
what was his name? I've forgotten. He would have been a child
when I came here from Clazomenae to stay before – and that's
a long time ago now. I think his father's name was Pyrilampes."

"It was, indeed," he said.

"And his?"

"Antiphon. But why do you ask?"

"These men are fellow citizens of mine," I said, "keen philosophers, and they have heard that this Antiphon met many times
with a friend of Zeno's called Pythodorus and can recite from   c
memory the discussion that Socrates and Zeno and Parmenides
once had, since he heard it often from Pythodorus."

"That's true," he said.

"Well, we want to hear that discussion," I replied.

"Nothing hard about that," he said. "When Antiphon was a
young man, he practiced it to perfection, although these days,
just like the grandfather he's named for, he devotes most of his
time to horses. But if that's what's called for, let's go to his
house. He left here to go home just a short time ago, but he
lives close by in Melite."

After this exchange, we set off walking and found Antiphon 127
at home engaging a smith to work on a bit of some kind. When

---

1. On the dramatic characters in the dialogue, see the sections in the
introduction entitled "The Frames" and "Parmenides and Zeno."

he had finished with the smith, and his brothers told him why we were there, he recognized me from my earlier visit and greeted me. We asked him to go through the discussion, and he balked at first – it was, he said, a lot of work. But finally he narrated it in detail.

Antiphon said that Pythodorus said that Zeno and Parmenides once came to the Great Panathenaea. Parmenides was already quite venerable, very gray but of distinguished appearance, about sixty-five years old. Zeno was at that time close to forty, a tall, handsome man who had been, as rumor had it, the object of Parmenides' affections when he was a boy. Antiphon said that the two of them were staying with Pythodorus, outside the city wall in the Potters' Quarter, and that Socrates had come there, along with a number of others, because they were eager to hear Zeno read his book, which he and Parmenides had just brought to Athens for the first time. Socrates was then quite young.

Zeno was reading to them in person; Parmenides happened to be out. Very little remained to be read when Pythodorus, as he related it, came in, and with him Parmenides and Aristotle – the man who later became one of the Thirty. They listened to a little of the book at the very end. But not Pythodorus himself; he had heard Zeno read it before.

Then Socrates, after he had heard it, asked Zeno to read the first hypothesis of the first argument again; and when he had read it, Socrates said, "Zeno, what do you mean by this: if things are many,[2] they must then be both like and unlike, but that is impossible, because unlike things can't be like or like things unlike? That's what you say, isn't it?"

"It is," said Zeno.

"If it's impossible for unlike things to be like and like things unlike, isn't it then also impossible for them to be many? Because, if they were many, they would have incompatible properties. Is this the point of your arguments – simply to maintain, in opposition to everything that is commonly said, that things are not many? And do you suppose that each of your arguments is proof for this position, so that you think you give as many proofs that

_b_

_c_

_d_

_e_

---

2. The Greek uses the phrase *ta onta*, literally "things that are," so the literal translation of Zeno's hypothesis is: "If things that are are many."

things are not many as your book has arguments? Is that what
you're saying – or do I misunderstand?"   *128*
"No," Zeno replied. "On the contrary, you grasp the general
point of the book splendidly."

"Parmenides," Socrates said, "I understand that Zeno wants
to be on intimate terms with you not only in friendship but also
in his book. He has, in a way, written the same thing as you,
but by changing it round he tries to fool us into thinking he is
saying something different. You say in your poem that the all
is one, and you give splendid and excellent proofs for that; he, *b*
for his part, says that it is not many and gives a vast array of
very grand proofs of his own. So, with one of you saying 'one,'
and the other 'not many,' and with each of you speaking in a
way that suggests that you've said nothing the same – although
you mean practically the same thing – what you've said you
appear to have said over the heads of the rest of us."

"Yes, Socrates," said Zeno. "Still, you haven't completely dis-
cerned the truth about my book, even though you chase down
its arguments and follow their spoor as keenly as a young Spartan *c*
hound. First of all, you have missed this point: the book doesn't
at all preen itself on having been written with the intent you
described, while disguising it from people, as if that were some
great accomplishment. You have mentioned something that happened accidentally. The truth is that the book comes to the
defense of Parmenides' argument against those who try to make
fun of it by claiming that, if it³ is one, many absurdities and self- *d*
contradictions result from that argument. Accordingly, my book
speaks against those who assert the many and pays them back
in kind with something for good measure, since it aims to make
clear that their hypothesis, if it is many,⁴ would, if someone

---

3. i.e., the all.
4. In English we normally speak of a hypothesis *that* something is the
case, even in contexts where the hypothesis is proposed for testing
through examination of its implications and consequences. Instead,
Zeno here, and later Socrates and Parmenides, regularly place the content of a hypothesis within an "if" clause (making it grammatically the
hypothesis *if*, rather than the hypothesis *that*, something is the case).
They are thinking of the hypothesis as placed before us in the form if-
then, ready for us to draw out its implications and consequences: e.g.,
"if the all is one, then . . . ," or "if the all is many, then. . . ."

examined the matter thoroughly, suffer consequences even more
absurd than those suffered by the hypothesis of its being one.
In that competitive spirit, then, I wrote the book when I was a
young man. Someone made an unauthorized copy, so I didn't
even have a chance to decide for myself whether or not it should
e   see the light. So in this respect you missed the point, Socrates:
you think it was written not out of a young man's competitive-
ness, but out of a mature man's vainglory. Still, as I said, your
portrayal was not bad."

"I take your point," Socrates said, "and I believe it was as you
say. But tell me this: don't you acknowledge that there is a form,
129 itself by itself,[5] of likeness, and another form, opposite to this,
which is what unlike is? Don't you and I and the other things
we call 'many' get a share of those two entities? And don't things
that get a share of likeness come to be like in that way and to
the extent that they get a share, whereas things that get a share
of unlikeness come to be unlike, and things that get a share of
both come to be both? And even if all things get a share of both,
though they are opposites, and by partaking of them are both
like and unlike themselves, what's astonishing about that?

b   "If someone showed that the likes themselves come to be
unlike or the unlikes like – that, I think, would be a marvel; but
if he shows that things that partake of both of these have both
properties, there seems to me nothing strange about that, Zeno –
not even if someone shows that all things are one by partaking
of oneness,[6] and that these same things are many by partaking

---

5. "Itself by itself," which translates the Greek phrase *auto kath hauto*,
is a technical expression for Plato. Our translation aims to capture the
variety of the expression's meaning, as understood by the speakers in
this dialogue. First, something is "itself by itself" if it is separate from
other things or is considered on its own, apart from other things. When
the phrase is construed in this way, "by itself" means "apart, on its
own." Second, something is "itself by itself," if it is itself responsible
for its own proper being, independently of other things. When the
phrase is understood in this way, "by itself" means "in virtue of, or
because of, itself." Both of these meanings should be kept in mind
whenever this phrase recurs in the translation.

6. Plato uses the expression *to hen* as the name of a form, and we
sometimes translate it as "the one" and sometimes as "oneness" (Aristotle seems to have been the first to introduce the abstract noun *henotes*

also of multitude.[7] But if he should demonstrate this thing itself, what one is, to be many, or, conversely, the many to be one – at this I'll be astonished.

"And it's the same with all the others: if he could show that the kinds and forms[8] themselves have in themselves these opposite properties, that would call for astonishment. But if someone should demonstrate that I am one thing and many, what's astonishing about that? He will say, when he wants to show that I'm many, that my right side is different from my left, and my front from my back, and likewise with my upper and lower parts – since I take it I do partake of multitude. But when he wants to show that I'm one, he will say I'm one person among the seven of us, because I also partake of oneness. Thus he shows that both are true.

"So if – in the case of stones and sticks and such things – someone tries to show that the same thing is many and one, we'll say that he is demonstrating *something* to be many and one,

c

d

---

for "oneness"). In the deductions concerning the one in the second part of the dialogue, much turns on the fact that *hen* or *to hen* can refer, not only to the form, but also to the number one, to any object that is one, and to the character a thing has if it is one. Furthermore, the adjective *hen* has various meanings. Something can be called "one" because it is a single thing or because it is a unified whole composed of parts. One aim of the dialogue is to show that "one" is used in various ways and to challenge us, the readers, to determine its use in particular contexts. Our English translation aims to preserve that challenge by using only "the one," "oneness," and "one" to translate the Greek term, leaving the reader to determine the referent and meaning from its use in each context.

7. Like *to hen*, the expression *plethos*, which we render throughout as "multitude," is also ambiguous. It can refer to a form, to any group of many things, or to the character things have if they are many. Corresponding to the ambiguity in the meaning of "one," between "single" and "unified," "multitude" can specify a plurality of definite individuals or some mass that lacks unity and definiteness.

8. In this dialogue Plato uses three different abstract expressions to specify forms, two of which occur here: *genos* (a term restricted to Part I of the dialogue), which we render as "kind," and *eidos*, which we render as "form." Later he will use a third term, *idea*, which we render as "character."

not the one to be many or the many one – and we'll say that he
is saying nothing astonishing, but just what all of us would agree
to. But if someone first distinguishes as separate the forms,
themselves by themselves, of the things I was talking about a
moment ago – for example, likeness and unlikeness, multitude
e   and oneness, rest and motion, and everything of that sort –
and then shows that in themselves they can mix together and
separate, I for my part," he said, "would be utterly amazed,
Zeno. I think these issues have been handled with great vigor
in your book; but I would, as I say, be much more impressed if
someone were able to display this same difficulty, which you
and Parmenides went through in the case of visible things, also
130 similarly entwined in multifarious ways in the forms themselves – in things that are grasped by reasoning."

Pythodorus said that, while Socrates was saying all this, he
himself kept from moment to moment expecting Parmenides
and Zeno to get annoyed; but they both paid close attention to
Socrates and often glanced at each other and smiled, as though
they admired him. In fact, what Parmenides said when Socrates
had finished confirmed this impression. "Socrates," he said,
b   "you are much to be admired for your keenness for argument!
Tell me. Have you yourself distinguished as separate, in the way
you mention, certain forms themselves, and also as separate the
things that partake of them? And do you think that likeness
itself is something, separate from the likeness we have? And
one and many and all the things you heard Zeno read about a
while ago?"

"I do indeed," Socrates answered.

"And what about these?" asked Parmenides. "Is there a form,
itself by itself, of just, and beautiful, and good, and everything
of that sort?"

"Yes," he said.

c   "What about a form of human being, separate from us and
all those like us? Is there a form itself of human being, or fire,
or water?"

Socrates said, "Parmenides, I've often found myself in doubt
whether I should talk about those in the same way as the others
or differently."

"And what about these, Socrates? Things that might seem
absurd, like hair and mud and dirt, or anything else totally

undignified and worthless? Are you doubtful whether or not you should say that a form is separate for each of these, too, *d* which in turn is other than anything we touch with our hands?"

"Not at all," Socrates answered. "On the contrary, these things are in fact just what we see. Surely it's too outlandish to think there is a form for them. Not that the thought that the same thing might hold in all cases hasn't troubled me from time to time. Then, when I get bogged down in that, I hurry away, afraid that I may fall into some pit of nonsense and come to harm; but when I arrive back in the vicinity of the things we agreed a moment ago have forms, I linger there and occupy myself with them."

"That's because you are still young, Socrates," said Parmen- *e* ides, "and philosophy has not yet gripped you as, in my opinion, it will in the future, once you begin to consider none of the cases beneath your notice. Now, though, you still care about what people think, because of your youth.

"But tell me this: is it your view that, as you say, there are certain forms from which these other things, by getting a share of them, derive their names – as, for instance, they come to be like by getting a share of likeness, large by getting a share of *131* largeness, and just and beautiful by getting a share of justice and beauty?"

"It certainly is," Socrates replied.

"So does each thing that gets a share get as its share the form as a whole or a part of it? Or could there be some other means of getting a share apart from these two?"

"How could there be?" he said.

"Do you think, then, that the form as a whole – one thing – is in each of the many? Or what do you think?"

"What's to prevent its being one, Parmenides?"[9] said Socrates.

"So, being one and the same, it will be at the same time, as *b* a whole, in things that are many and separate; and thus it would be separate from itself."

---

9. We retain the manuscript reading, which Burnet brackets in the Oxford text. The translation of Burnet's text would be simply: "What's to prevent it, Parmenides?"

"No it wouldn't," Socrates said. "Not if it's like one and the same day. That is in many places at the same time and is none the less not separate from itself. If it's like that, each of the forms might be, at the same time, one and the same in all."

"Socrates," he said, "how neatly you make one and the same thing be in many places at the same time! It's as if you were to cover many people with a sail, and then say that one thing as a whole is over many. Or isn't that the sort of thing you mean to say?"

c   "Perhaps," he replied.

"In that case would the sail be, as a whole, over each person, or would a part of it be over one person and another part over another?"

"A part."

"So the forms themselves are divisible, Socrates," he said, "and things that partake of them would partake of a part; no longer would a whole form, but only a part of it, be in each thing."

"It does appear that way."

"Then are you willing to say, Socrates, that our one form is really divided? Will it still be one?"

"Not at all," he replied.

"No," said Parmenides. "For suppose you are going to divide
d   largeness itself. If each of the many large things is to be large by a part of largeness smaller than largeness itself, won't that appear unreasonable?"

"It certainly will," he replied.

"What about this? Will each thing that has received a small part of the equal have something by which to be equal to anything, when its portion is less than the equal itself?"

"That's impossible."

"Well, suppose one of us is going to have a part of the small. The small will be larger than that part of it, since the part is a part of it: so the small itself will be larger! And that to which
e   the part subtracted is added will be smaller, not larger, than it was before."

"That surely couldn't happen," he said.

"Socrates, in what way, then, will the other things get a share of your forms, if they can do so neither by getting parts nor by getting wholes?"

"By Zeus!" Socrates exclaimed. "It strikes me that's not at all easy to determine!"

"And what do you think about the following?"

"What's that?"

"I suppose you think each form is one on the following ground: *132* whenever some number of things seem to you to be large, perhaps there seems to be some one character,[10] the same as you look at them all, and from that you conclude that the large is one."

"That's true," he said.

"What about the large itself and the other large things? If you look at them all in the same way with the mind's eye, again won't some one thing appear large, by which all these appear large?"[11]

"It seems so."

"So another form of largeness will make its appearance, which has emerged alongside largeness itself and the things that partake of it, and in turn another over all these, by which all of *b* them will be large. Each of your forms will no longer be one, but unlimited in multitude."

"But, Parmenides, maybe each of these forms is a thought,"[12] Socrates said, "and properly occurs only in minds. In this way each of them might be one and no longer face the difficulties mentioned just now."

---

10. Plato here uses the expression *idea*, which we render as "character." He will use this expression in the arguments that follow as an alternative to *genos* ("kind") and *eidos* ("form") in reference to forms (see n.8 above). Here in its first occurrence, however, the word probably refers, not to a form, but to the common character Socrates takes various things to have, if they all seem to be large (cf. "the likeness we have," contrasted with "likeness itself," at 130b). We avoid the traditional translation "idea" for Plato's word, because Platonic forms are not mental entities. The technical use of "idea" in the later history of philosophy is misleading in the Platonic context.

11. This sentence can also be translated: "If you look at them all in the same way with the mind's eye, won't some one large again appear, by which all these appear large?"

12. This sentence is ambiguous in the Greek. It can also be translated: "But, Parmenides, maybe each of the forms is a thought of these things."

"What do you mean?" he asked. "Is each of the thoughts one, but a thought of nothing?"

"No, that's impossible," he said.

"Of something, rather?"

"Yes."

c   "Of something that is, or of something that is not?"

"Of something that is."

"Isn't it of some one thing, which that thought thinks is over all the instances, being some one character?"

"Yes."

"Then won't this thing that is thought to be one, being always the same over all the instances, be a form?"

"That, too, appears necessary."

"And what about this?" said Parmenides. "Given your claim that other things partake of forms, won't you necessarily think either that each thing is composed of thoughts and all things think, or that, although they are thoughts, they are un-thinking?"[13]

"That isn't reasonable either, Parmenides," he said. "No, what
d   appears most likely to me is this: these forms are like patterns set in nature, and other things resemble them and are likenesses; and this partaking of the forms is, for the other things, simply being modeled on them."

"If something resembles the form," he said, "can that form not be like what has been modeled on it, to the extent that the thing has been made like it? Or is there any way for something like to be like what is not like it?"

"There is not."

"And isn't there a compelling necessity for that which is like
e   to partake of the same one form as what is like it?"[14]

"There is."

"But if like things are like by partaking of something, won't that be the form itself?"

---

13. The second alternative could also be translated: "or that, although they are thoughts, they are not thought."

14. We follow the manuscript reading, which Burnet brackets in the Oxford text. If *eidous* ("form") is excised, the translation is: "And isn't there a compelling necessity for that which is like to partake of the same one thing as what is like it?"

"Undoubtedly."

"Therefore nothing can be like the form, nor can the form be like anything else. Otherwise, alongside the form another form will always make its appearance, and if that form is like anything, 133 yet another; and if the form proves to be like what partakes of it, a fresh form will never cease emerging."

"That's very true."

"So other things don't get a share of the forms by likeness; we must seek some other means by which they get a share."

"So it seems."

"Then do you see, Socrates," he said, "how great the difficulty is if one marks things off as forms, themselves by themselves?"[15]

"Quite clearly."

"I assure you," he said, "that you do not yet, if I may put it so, have an inkling of how great the difficulty is if you are going _b_ to posit one form in each case every time you make a distinction among things."

"How so?" he asked.

"There are many other reasons," Parmenides said, "but the main one is this: suppose someone were to say that if the forms are such as we claim they must be, they cannot even be known. If anyone should raise that objection, you wouldn't be able to show him that he is wrong, unless the objector happened to be widely experienced and not ungifted, and consented to pay attention while in your effort to show him you dealt with many distant considerations. Otherwise, the person who insists that they are necessarily unknowable would remain unconvinced." _c_

"Why is that, Parmenides?" Socrates asked.

"Because I think that you, Socrates, and anyone else who posits that there is for each thing some being, itself by itself, would agree, to begin with, that none of those beings is in us."[16]

"Yes – how could it still be itself by itself?" replied Socrates.

"Very good," said Parmenides. "And so all the characters that are what they are in relation to each other have their being in relation to themselves but not in relation to things that belong

---

15. On the phrase "themselves by themselves," see n.5 above.

16. For Parmenides' previous use of the phrase "in us," cf. 131a. For mention of properties we have, separate from the corresponding forms, cf. 130b.

d   to us. And whether one posits these[17] as likenesses or in some
     other way, it is by partaking of them that we come to be called
     by their various names. These things that belong to us, although
     they have the same names as the forms, are in their turn what
     they are in relation to themselves but not in relation to the forms;
     and all the things named in this way are *of* themselves but not
     of the forms."

        "What do you mean?" Socrates asked.

        "Take an example," said Parmenides. "If one of us is some-
     body's master or somebody's slave, he is surely not a slave of
e   master itself – of what a master is – nor is the master a master
     of slave itself – of what a slave is. On the contrary, being a
     human being, he is a master or slave of a human being. Mastery
     itself, on the other hand, is what it is of slavery itself; and, in
     the same way, slavery itself is slavery of mastery itself. Things
     in us do not have their power in relation to forms, nor do they
     have theirs in relation to us; but, I repeat, forms are what they
     are *of* themselves and in relation to themselves, and things that
134 belong to us are, in the same way, what they are in relation to
     themselves. You do understand what I mean?"

        "Certainly," Socrates said, "I understand."

        "So too," he said, "knowledge itself, what knowledge is,
     would be knowledge of that truth itself, which is what truth is?"

        "Certainly."

        "Furthermore, each particular knowledge, what it is, would
     be knowledge of some particular thing, of what that thing is.
     Isn't that so?"

        "Yes."

        "But wouldn't knowledge that belongs to us be of the truth
     that belongs to our world?[18] And wouldn't it follow that each

---

17. i.e., the things that belong to us.

18. In this argument Parmenides has been using two phrases in a
semitechnical way: *en hemin*, which we render as "in us," and *par hemin*,
which we have so far rendered as "belong(s) to us." That translation
cannot be maintained consistently in what follows, because Parmenides
begins to apply the phrase, as here, to truths or things that belong to
our physical world. In the remainder of this argument we therefore
translate *par hemin* sometimes as "belong(s) to us" and sometimes as
"belong(s) to our world" or "in our world."

particular knowledge that belongs to us is in turn knowledge of   *b*
some particular thing in our world?"

"Necessarily."

"But, as you agree, we neither have the forms themselves nor
can they belong to us."

"Yes, you're quite right."

"And surely the kinds themselves, what each of them is, are
known by the form of knowledge itself?"

"Yes."

"The very thing that we don't have."

"No, we don't."

"So none of the forms is known by us, because we don't
partake of knowledge itself."

"It seems not."

"Then the beautiful itself, what it is, cannot be known by us,
nor can the good, nor, indeed, can any of the things we take to   *c*
be characters themselves."

"It looks that way."

"Here's something even more shocking than that."

"What's that?"

"Surely you would say that if in fact there is knowledge – a
kind itself – it is much more precise than is knowledge that
belongs to us. And the same goes for beauty and all the others."

"Yes."

"Well, whatever else partakes of knowledge itself, wouldn't
you say that god more than anyone else has this most precise
knowledge?"

"Necessarily."

"Tell me, will god, having knowledge itself, then be able to   *d*
know things that belong to our world?"

"Yes, why not?"

"Because we have agreed, Socrates," Parmenides said, "that
those forms do not have their power in relation to things in our
world, and things in our world do not have theirs in relation to
forms, but that things in each group have their power in relation
to themselves."

"Yes, we did agree on that."

"Well then, if this most precise mastery and this most precise
knowledge belong to the divine, the gods' mastery could never
master us, nor could their knowledge know us or anything that   *e*

belongs to us. No, just as we do not govern them by our gover-
nance and know nothing of the divine by our knowledge, so
they in their turn are, for the same reason, neither our masters
nor, being gods, do they know human affairs."

"If god is to be stripped of knowing," he said, "our argument
may be getting too bizarre."

"And yet, Socrates," said Parmenides, "the forms inevitably
135 involve these objections and a host of others besides – if there
are those characters for things, and a person is to mark off each
form as 'something itself.' As a result, whoever hears about them
is doubtful and objects that they do not exist, and that, even if
they *do*, they must by strict necessity be unknowable to human
nature; and in saying this he seems to have a point; and, as we
said, he is extraordinarily hard to win over. Only a very gifted
man can come to know that for each thing there is some kind,
b   a being itself by itself; but only a prodigy more remarkable still
will discover that and be able to teach someone else who has
sifted all these difficulties thoroughly and critically for himself."

"I agree with you, Parmenides," Socrates said. "That's very
much what I think too."

"Yet on the other hand, Socrates," said Parmenides, "if someone, having an eye on all the difficulties we have just brought
up and others of the same sort, won't allow that there are forms
for things and won't mark off a form for each one, he won't
have anywhere to turn his thought, since he doesn't allow that
c   for each thing there is a character that is always the same. In
this way he will destroy the power of dialectic[19] entirely. But I
think you are only too well aware of that."

"What you say is true," Socrates said.

"What then will you do about philosophy? Where will you
turn, while these difficulties remain unresolved?"

"I don't think I have anything clearly in view, at least not at
present."

"Socrates, that's because you are trying to mark off something
beautiful, and just, and good, and each one of the forms, too
soon," he said, "before you have been properly trained. I noticed

---

19. The Greek word is *dialegesthai*, which could instead be translated as
"discourse," or untechnically as "conversation."

that the other day too, as I listened to you conversing[20] with   *d*
Aristotle here. The impulse you bring to argument is noble and
divine, make no mistake about it. But while you are still young,
put your back into it and get more training through something
people think useless – what the crowd call idle talk. Otherwise,
the truth will escape you."

"What manner of training is that, Parmenides?" he asked.

"The manner is just what you heard from Zeno," he said.
"Except I was also impressed by something you had to say to   *e*
him: you didn't allow him to remain among visible things and
observe their wandering between opposites. You asked him to
observe it instead among those things that one might above all
grasp by means of reason and might think to be forms."

"I did that," he said, "because I think that here, among visible
things, it's not at all hard to show that things are both like and
unlike and anything else you please."

"And you are quite right," he said. "But you must do the
following in addition to that: if you want to be trained more
thoroughly, you must not only hypothesize, if each thing is,
and examine the consequences of that hypothesis; you must also *136*
hypothesize, if that same thing is not."

"What do you mean?" he asked.

"If you like," said Parmenides, "take as an example this hypothesis that Zeno entertained: if many are,[21] what must the
consequences be both for the many themselves in relation to
themselves and in relation to the one, and for the one in relation
to itself and in relation to the many? And, in turn, on the hypothesis, if many are not, you must again examine what the consequences will be both for the one and for the many in relation to
themselves and in relation to each other. And again, in turn, if   *b*
you hypothesize, if likeness is or if it is not, you must examine
what the consequences will be on each hypothesis, both for

---

20. The Greek participle is *dialegomenou*. See previous note.

21. See n.4 above on "hypothesis." The meaning of the Greek phrase
ei polla esti is underdetermined. We have rendered it as "if many are,"
with "many" as subject. But "many" could instead be the predicate
with a subject understood ("if [things] are many"). See the introduction,
the sections entitled "Plan of the Deductions" and "The Positive Hypothesis."

the things hypothesized themselves and for the others, both in relation to themselves and in relation to each other. And the same method applies to unlike, to motion, to rest, to generation and destruction, and to being itself and not-being. And, in a word, concerning whatever you might ever hypothesize as being or as not being or as having any other property, you must examine the consequences for the thing you hypothesize in relation
c   to itself and in relation to each one of the others, whichever you select, and in relation to several of them and to all of them in the same way; and, in turn, you must examine the others, both in relation to themselves and in relation to whatever other thing you select on each occasion, whether what you hypothesize you hypothesize as being or as not being. All this you must do if, after completing your training, you are to achieve a full view of the truth."

"Scarcely manageable, Parmenides, this task you describe! And besides, I don't quite understand," he said. "To help me understand more fully, why don't you hypothesize something and go through the exercise for me yourself?"

d   "For a man my age that's a big assignment, Socrates," he said.

"Well then," said Socrates, "you, Zeno – why don't you go through it for us?"

And Antiphon said that Zeno laughed and said, "Let's beg Parmenides to do it himself, Socrates. What he's proposing won't be easy, I'm afraid. Or don't you recognize what a big assignment it is? Indeed, if there were more of us here, it wouldn't be right to ask him – it's not fitting, especially for a man his age, to engage in such a discussion in front of a crowd. Ordinary people
e   don't know that without this comprehensive and circuitous treatment we cannot hit upon the truth and gain insight. And so, Parmenides, I join with Socrates in begging you, so that I too may become your pupil again after all this time."

When Zeno had finished speaking, Antiphon said that Pythodorus said that he too, along with Aristotle and the others, begged Parmenides not to refuse, but to give a demonstration of what he was recommending. In the end Parmenides said: "I am obliged to go along with you. And yet I feel like the horse in the poem of Ibycus.[22] Ibycus compares himself to a horse – a

---

22. Ibycus frag. 6 (Page 1962). Ibycus of Rhegium, who—like Parmen-

champion but no longer young, on the point of drawing a chariot 137
in a race and trembling at what experience tells him is about to
happen – and says that he himself, old man that he is, is being
forced against his will to compete in Love's game. I too, when
I think back, feel a good deal of anxiety as to how at my age I
am to make my way across such a vast and formidable sea of
words. Even so, I'll do it, since it is right for me to oblige you;
and besides, we are, as Zeno says, by ourselves.

"Well then, at what point shall we start? What shall we hypoth- b
esize first? I know: since we have in fact decided to play this
strenuous game, is it all right with you if I begin with myself
and my own hypothesis? Shall I hypothesize about the one itself
and consider what the consequences must be, if it is one or if it
is not one?"[23]

"By all means," said Zeno.

"Then who will answer my questions?" he asked. "The youngest, surely? For he would give the least trouble and would be
the most likely to say what he thinks. At the same time his
answer would allow me a breathing space."

"I'm ready to play this role for you, Parmenides," Aristotle c
said. "Because you mean me when you say the youngest. Ask
away – you can count on me to answer."

Deduction 1

"Very good," he said. "If it is one,[24] the one would not be many,
would it?"—"No, how could it?"—"Then there cannot be a part
of it nor can it be a whole."—"Why?"—"A part is surely part of
a whole."—"Yes."—"But what is the whole? Wouldn't that from

---

ides—was a native of one of the Western Greek colonies in Italy, was
known in antiquity as a poet of love. He flourished in the second half
of the sixth century B.C. at the court of the tyrant Polycrates on the
Ionian island of Samos.

23. The Greek is *eite hen estin eite me hen*. Some scholars have proposed
emending the text so that they can translate: "if one is or if it is not."
24. The Greek is underdetermined: the hypothesis could be rendered
as "if it is one," or "if one is." Cf. Parmenides' statement above at 137b.
For a discussion of the translation, see the introduction, the section
entitled "The Positive Hypothesis."

which no part is missing be a whole?"—"Certainly."—"In both cases, then, the one would be composed of parts, both if it is a whole and if it has parts."—"Necessarily."—"So in both cases

d the one would thus be many rather than one."—"True."—"Yet it must be not many but one."—"It must."—"Therefore, if the one is to be one, it will neither be a whole nor have parts."— "No, it won't."

"Well, then, if it doesn't have a part, it could have neither a beginning nor an end nor a middle; for those would in fact be parts of it."—"That's right."—"Furthermore, end and beginning are limits of each thing."—"Doubtless."—"So the one is unlimited if it has neither beginning nor end."—"Unlimited."—"So it is also without shape; for it partakes of neither round nor

e straight."—"How so?"—"Round is surely that whose extremities are equidistant in every direction from the middle."—"Yes."— "Furthermore, straight is that whose middle stands in the way of the two extremities."—"Just so."—"So the one would have parts and be many if it partook of either a straight or a curved shape."—"Of course."—"Therefore it is neither straight nor

138 curved, since in fact it doesn't have parts."—"That's right."

"Furthermore, being like that, it would be nowhere, because it could be neither in another nor in itself."—"How is that?"— "If it were in another, it would surely be contained all around by the thing it was in and would touch it in many places with many parts; but since it is one and without parts and does not partake of circularity, it cannot possibly touch in many places all around."—"It can't."—"Yet, on the other hand, if it were in itself, its container would be none other than itself, if in fact it

b were in itself; for a thing can't be in something that doesn't contain it."—"No, it can't."—"So the container itself would be one thing, and the thing contained something else, since the same thing will not, as a whole at any rate, undergo and do both at once. And in that case the one would be no longer one but two."—"Yes, you're quite right."—"Therefore, the one is not anywhere, if it is neither in itself nor in another."—"It isn't."

"Then consider whether, since it is as we have said, it can be at rest or in motion."—"Yes, why not?"—"Because if it moves, it would either move spatially or be altered, since these are the

c only motions."—"Yes."—"But the one surely can't be altered from itself and still be one."—"It can't."—"Then it doesn't move by alteration at least."—"Apparently not."—"But by moving spatially?"—"Perhaps."—"And if the one moved spatially, it surely would either spin in a circle in the same location or change from one place to another."—"Necessarily."—"Well then, if it spins in a circle, it must be poised on its middle and have other parts of itself that move round the middle. But how will a thing that has nothing to do with middle or parts manage to be moved   d in a circle round its middle?"—"Not at all."—"But by changing places does it come to be here at one time, there at another, and move in this way?"—"If in fact it moves at all."—"Wasn't it shown that it cannot be anywhere in anything?"—"Yes."— "Then is it not even more impossible for it to *come* to be?"—"I don't see why."—"If something comes to be in something, isn't it necessary that it not yet be in that thing – since it is still coming to be in it – and that it no longer be entirely outside it, if in fact it is already coming to be in it?"—"Necessarily."—"So if anything is to undergo this, only that which has parts could do so, because   e some of it would already be in that thing, while some, at the same time, would be outside. But a thing that doesn't have parts will not by any means be able to be, at the same time, neither wholly inside nor wholly outside something."—"True."—"But isn't it much more impossible still for a thing that has no parts and is not a whole to come to be in something somewhere, if it does so neither part by part nor as a whole?"—"Apparently."— "Therefore it doesn't change places by going somewhere and coming to be in something, nor does it move by spinning in the 139 same location or by being altered."—"It seems not."—"The one, therefore, is unmoved by every sort of motion."—"Unmoved."

"Yet, on the other hand, we also say that it cannot be in anything."—"Yes, we do."—"Then it is also never in the *same* thing."—"Why?"—"Because it would then be *in* that – in that same thing it is in."—"Of course."—"But it was impossible for it to be either in itself or in another."—"Yes, you're quite right."—"So the one is never in the same thing."—"It seems not."—"But what is never in the same thing neither enjoys re-   b pose nor is at rest."—"No, it cannot."—"Therefore the one, as it seems, is neither at rest nor in motion."—"It certainly does appear not."

"Furthermore, it won't be the same as another thing or itself; nor, again, could it be different from itself or another thing."—

"Why is that?"—"If it were different from itself, it would surely be different from one, and would not be one."—"True."—"On the other hand, if it were the same as another, it would be that
c   thing, and not itself. So in this way, too, it would not be just what it is – one – but would be different from one."—"Yes, you're quite right."—"Therefore, it won't be the same as another or different from itself."—"No, it won't."

"And it won't be different from another, as long as it is one; for it is not proper to one to be different from something, but proper to different-from-another alone, and to nothing else."—"That's right."—"Therefore it won't be different by being one. Or do you think it will?"—"No indeed."—"Yet if it isn't different by being one, it will not be so by itself; and if it isn't so by itself, it will not itself be so. And if it is itself in no way different, it will be different from nothing."—"That's right."

d   "Nor will it be the same as itself."—"Why not?"—"The nature of the one is not, of course, also that of the same."—"Why?"— "Because it is not the case that, whenever a thing comes to be the same as something, it comes to be one."—"But why?"—"If it comes to be the same as the many, it must come to be many, not one."—"True."—"But if the one and the same in no way differ, whenever something came to be the same, it would always come to be one; and whenever it came to be one, it would always
e   come to be the same."—"Certainly."—"Therefore, if the one is to be the same as itself, it won't be one with itself; and thus it will be one and not one. But this surely is impossible. Therefore the one can't be either different from another or the same as itself."—"It can't."—"Thus the one could neither be different from nor the same as itself or another."—"Yes, you're quite right."

"Furthermore, it will be neither like nor unlike anything, either itself or another."—"Why?"—"Because whatever has a property the same is surely like."—"Yes."—"But it was shown that the same is separate in its nature from the one."—"Yes, it was."—
140 "But if the one has any property apart from being one, it would be more than one; and that is impossible."—"Yes."—"Therefore, the one can in no way have a property the same as another or itself."—"Apparently not."—"So it cannot be like another or itself either."—"It seems not."

"Nor does the one have the property of being different; for in this way too it would be more than one."—"Yes, it would be

more."—"Surely that which has a property different from itself
or another would be unlike itself or another, if in fact what has
a property the same is like."—"That's right."—"But the one, as   *b*
it seems, since it in no way has a property different, is in no
way unlike itself or another thing."—"Yes, you're quite right."—
"Therefore the one could be neither like nor unlike another or
itself."—"Apparently not."

"Furthermore, being like that, it will be neither equal nor
unequal to itself or another."—"How?"—"If it is equal, it will
be of the same measures as that to which it is equal."—"Yes."—
"But surely if it is greater or less, it will, in the case of things
with which it is commensurate, have more measures than those   *c*
that are less, and fewer than those that are greater."—"Yes."—
"And in the case of things with which it is not commensurate,
it will be of smaller measures in the one case, and of larger
measures in the other."—"No doubt."—"Well, if a thing doesn't
partake of the same, it can't be of the same measures or of the
same anything else at all, can it?"—"It can't."—"So it couldn't
be equal to itself or another, if it is not of the same measures."—
"It certainly appears not."—"Yet if it is, on the other hand, of
more measures or fewer, it would have as many parts as measures; and thus, again, it will be no longer one, but just as many   *d*
as are its measures."—"That's right."—"And if it were of one
measure, it would prove to be equal to its measure; but it was
shown that it couldn't be equal to anything."—"Yes, it was."—
"Therefore, since it doesn't partake of one measure or many or
few, and since it doesn't partake of the same at all, it will, as it
seems, never be equal to itself or another; nor again will it be
greater or less than itself or another."—"That's absolutely so."

"What about this? Do you think that the one can be older or   *e*
younger than, or the same age as, anything?"—"Yes, why
not?"—"Because if it is the same age as itself or another, it will
surely partake of likeness and of equality of time, of which –
likeness and equality – we said the one has no share."—"Yes,
we did say that."—"And we also said that it does not partake
of unlikeness and inequality."—"Of course."—"Then, being like
that, how will it be able to be older or younger than, or the same   *141*
age as, anything?"—"In no way."—"Therefore, the one could
not be younger or older than, or the same age as, itself or another."—"Apparently not."

"So if it is like that, the one could not even be in time at all, could it? Or isn't it necessary, if something is in time, that it always come to be older than itself?"—"Necessarily."—"Isn't the older always older than a younger?"—"To be sure."—

b   "Therefore, that which comes to be older than itself comes to be, at the same time, younger than itself, if in fact it is to have something it comes to be older than."—"What do you mean?"— "I mean this: there is no need for a thing to come to be different from a thing that is already different; it must, rather, already be different from what is already different, have come to be different from what has come to be different, and be going to be different from what is going to be different; but it must not have come to be, be going to be, or be different from what comes to be different: it must come to be different, and nothing else."—

c   "Yes, that's necessary."—"But surely older is a difference from younger and from nothing else."—"Yes, it is."—"So that which comes to be older than itself must also, at the same time, come to be younger than itself."—"So it seems."—"But it must also not come to be for more or less time than itself; it must come to be and be and have come to be and be going to be for a time equal to itself."—"Yes, that too is necessary."—"Therefore it is necessary, as it seems, that each thing that is in time and partakes

d   of time be the same age as itself and, at the same time, come to be both older and younger than itself."—"It looks that way."— "But the one surely had no share of any of that."—"No, it didn't."—"Therefore, it has no share of time, nor is it *in* any time."—"It certainly isn't, as the argument proves."

"Now, don't you think that 'was' and 'has come to be' and 'was coming to be' signify partaking of time past?"—"By all

e   means."—"And again that 'will be' and 'will come to be' and 'will be coming to be' signify partaking of time hereafter?"— "Yes."—"And that 'is' and 'comes to be' signify partaking of time now present?"—"Of course."—"Therefore, if the one partakes of no time at all, it is not the case that it has at one time come to be, was coming to be, or was; or has now come to be, comes to be, or is; or will hereafter come to be, will be coming to be, or will be."—"Very true."—"Could something partake of being except in one of those ways?"—"It couldn't."—"Therefore the one in no way partakes of being."—"It seems not."—"Therefore the one in no way is."—"Apparently not."—"Therefore neither *is* it in such a way as to be one, because it would then, by being and partaking of being, be. But, as it seems, the one neither is one nor is, if we are obliged to trust this argument."—"It looks that way."   142

"If something is not, could anything belong *to* this thing that is not, or be *of* it?"—"How could it?"—"Therefore, no name belongs to it, nor is there an account or any knowledge or perception or opinion of it."—"Apparently not."—"Therefore it is not named or spoken of, nor is it the object of opinion or knowledge, nor does anything that is perceive it."—"It seems not."—"Is it possible that these things are so for the one?"—"I certainly don't think so."

Deduction 2

"Do you want to return to the hypothesis from the beginning,   *b* in the hope that another kind of result may come to light as we go back over it?"—"I do indeed."—"If one is, we are saying, aren't we, that we must agree on the consequences for it, whatever they happen to be?"—"Yes."—"Consider from the beginning: if one is, can it *be*, but not partake of being?"—"It cannot."—"So there would also be the being of the one, and that is not the same as the one. For if it were, it couldn't be the being of the one, nor could the one partake of it. On the contrary,   *c* saying that one is would be like saying that one is one.[25] But this time that is not the hypothesis, namely, what the consequences must be, if one is one, but if one is. Isn't that so?"— "Of course."—"Is that because 'is' signifies something other than 'one'?"—"Necessarily."—"So whenever someone, being brief, says 'one is,' would this simply mean that the one partakes of being?"—"Certainly."

"Let's again say what the consequences will be, if one is. Consider whether this hypothesis must not signify that the one is such as to have parts."—"How so?"—"In this way: if we state   *d* the 'is' of the one that is, and the 'one' of that which is one, and if being and oneness are not the same, but both belong to that

---

25. The Greek is *hen hen*, which could be translated as "one one." Our translation relies on the fact that the Greek verb "is," when used as a copula, is frequently omitted. Cf. also "if one is one" (*ei hen hen*) in the next sentence.

same thing that we hypothesized, namely, the one that is, must it not itself, since it is one being, be a whole, and the parts of this whole be oneness and being?"—"Necessarily."—"Shall we call each of these two parts a part only, or must the part be called part of the whole?"—"Of the whole."—"Therefore whatever is one both is a whole and has a part."—"Certainly."

    "Now, what about each of these two parts of the one that is,
e oneness and being? Is oneness ever absent from the being part or being from the oneness part?"—"That couldn't be."—"So again, each of the two parts possesses oneness and being; and the part, in its turn, is composed of at least two parts; and in this way always, for the same reason, whatever part turns up always possesses these two parts, since oneness always possesses being and being always possesses oneness. So, since it
143 always proves to be two, it must never be one."—"Absolutely."—"So, in this way, wouldn't the one that is be unlimited in multitude?"—"So it seems."

    "Come, let's proceed further in the following way."—"How?"—"Do we say that the one partakes of being, and hence is?"—"Yes."—"And for this reason the one that is was shown to be many."—"Just so."—"And what about the one itself, which we say partakes of being? If we grasp it in thought alone by itself, without that of which we say it partakes, will it appear to be only one, or will this same thing also appear to be many?"—
b "One, I should think."—"Let's see. Must not its being be something and it itself something different, if in fact the one is not being but, as one, partakes of being?"—"Necessarily."—"So if being is something and the one is something different, it is not by its being one that the one is different from being, nor by its being being that being is other than the one. On the contrary, they are different from each other by difference and otherness."—"Of course."—"And so difference is not the same as oneness or being."—"Obviously not."

c   "Now, if we select from them, say, being and difference, or being and oneness, or oneness and difference, do we not in each selection choose a certain pair that is correctly called 'both'?"—"How so?"—"As follows: we can say 'being'?"—"We can."—"And, again, we can say 'one'?"—"That too."—"So hasn't each of the pair been mentioned?"—"Yes."—"What about when I say 'being and oneness'? Haven't both been mentioned?"—"Certainly."—"And if I say 'being and difference' or 'difference and oneness,' and so on – in each case don't I speak of both?"— "Yes."—"Can things that are correctly called 'both' be both, but *d* not two?"—"They cannot."—"If there are two things, is there any way for each member of the pair not to be one?"—"Not at all."—"Therefore, since in fact each pair taken together turns out to be two, each member would be one."—"Apparently."— "And if each of them is one, when any one is added to any couple, doesn't the total prove to be three?"—"Yes."—"And isn't three odd, and two even?"—"Doubtless."

"What about this? Since there are two, must there not also be twice, and since there are three, thrice, if in fact two is two times *e* one and three is three times one?"—"Necessarily."—"Since there are two and twice, must there not be two times two? And since there are three and thrice, must there not be three times three?"—"Doubtless."—"And again: if there are three and they are two times, and if there are two and they are three times, must there not be two times three and three times two?"—"There certainly must."—"Therefore, there would be even times even, odd times odd, odd times even, and even times odd."—"That's *144* so."—"Then if that is so, do you think there is any number that need not be?"—"In no way at all."—"Therefore, if one is, there must also be number."—"Necessarily."—"But if there is number, there would be many, and an unlimited multitude of beings. Or doesn't number, unlimited in multitude, also prove to partake of being?"—"It certainly does."—"So if all number partakes of being, each part of number would also partake of it?"—"Yes."

"So has being been distributed to all things, which are many, *b* and is it missing from none of the beings, neither the smallest nor the largest? Or is it unreasonable even to ask that question? How could being be missing from any of the beings?"—"In no way."—"So being is chopped up into beings of all kinds, from the smallest to the largest possible, and is the most divided thing of all; and the parts of being are countless."—"Quite so."— *c* "Therefore its parts are the most numerous of things."—"The most numerous indeed."

"Now, is there any of them that is part of being, yet not one part?"—"How could that happen?"—"I take it, on the contrary, that if in fact it *is*, it must always, as long as it is, be some one thing; it cannot be nothing."—"Necessarily."—"So oneness is attached to every part of being and is not absent from a smaller or a larger, or any other, part."—"Just so."—"So, being one, is

d   it, as a whole, in many places at the same time? Look at this carefully."—"I am – and I see that it's impossible."—"Therefore as divided, if in fact not as a whole; for surely it will be present to all the parts of being at the same time only as divided."— "Yes."—"Furthermore, a divided thing certainly must be as numerous as its parts."—"Necessarily."—"So we were not speaking truly just now, when we said that being had been distributed into the most numerous parts. It is not distributed into more parts than oneness, but, as it seems, into parts equal to oneness,

e   since neither is being absent from oneness, nor is oneness absent from being. On the contrary, being two, they are always equal throughout all things."—"It appears absolutely so."—"Therefore, the one itself, chopped up by being, is many and unlimited in multitude."—"Apparently."—"So not only is it the case that the one being is many, but also the one itself, completely distributed by being, must be many."—"Absolutely."

"Furthermore, because the parts are parts of a whole, the one, as the whole, would be limited. Or aren't the parts contained by

145   the whole?"—"Necessarily."—"But surely that which contains would be a limit."—"Doubtless."—"So the one that is is surely both one and many, a whole and parts, and limited and unlimited in multitude."—"Apparently."

"So, since in fact it is limited, does it not also have extremities?"—"Necessarily."—"And again: if it is a whole, would it not have a beginning, a middle, and an end? Or can anything be a whole without those three? And if any one of them is missing from something, will it still consent to be a whole?"— "It won't."—"The one, as it seems, would indeed have a begin-

b   ning, an end, and a middle."—"It would."—"But the middle is equidistant from the extremities – otherwise, it wouldn't be a middle."—"No, it wouldn't."—"Since the one is like that, it would partake of some shape, as it seems, either straight or round, or some shape mixed from both."—"Yes, it would partake of a shape."

"Since it is so, won't it be both in itself and in another?"— "How so?"—"Each of the parts is surely in the whole, and none outside the whole."—"Just so."—"And are all the parts con-

c   tained by the whole?"—"Yes."—"Furthermore, the one is all the parts of itself, and not any more or less than all."—"No, it isn't."—"The one is also the whole, is it not?"—"Doubtless."—"So if all its parts are actually in a whole, and the one is both all the parts and the whole itself, and all the parts are contained by the whole, the one would be contained by the one; and thus the one itself would, then, be in itself."—"Apparently."

"Yet, on the other hand, the whole is not in the parts, in all or in some one. For if it were in all, it would also have to be in   *d* one, because if it were not in some one, it certainly could not be in all. And if this one is among them all, but the whole is not in it, how will the whole still be in all?"—"In no way."—"Nor is it in some of the parts: for if the whole were in some, the greater would be in the less, which is impossible."—"Yes, impossible."—"But if the whole is not in some or one or all the parts, must it not be in something different or be nowhere at all?"—"Necessarily."—"If it were nowhere, it would be nothing;   *e* but since it is a whole, and is not in itself, it must be in another. Isn't that so?"—"Certainly."—"So the one, insofar as it is a whole, is in another; but insofar as it is all the parts, it is in itself. And thus the one must be both in itself and in a different thing."—"Necessarily."

"Since that is the one's natural state, must it not be both in motion and at rest?"—"How?"—"It is surely at rest, if in fact it is in itself. For being in one thing and not stirring from that, it   146 would be in the same thing, namely, itself."—"Yes, it is."—"And that which is always in the same thing must, of course, always be at rest."—"Certainly."—"What about this? Must not that which is always in a different thing be, on the contrary, never in the same thing? And since it is never in the same thing, also not at rest? And since not at rest, in motion?"—"Just so."—"Therefore the one, since it is itself always both in itself and in a different thing, must always be both in motion and at rest."—"Apparently."

"Furthermore, it must be the same as itself and different from itself, and, likewise, the same as and different from the others,   *b* if in fact it has the aforesaid properties."—"How so?"—"Everything is surely related to everything as follows: either it is the same or different; or, if it is not the same or different, it would be related as part to whole or as whole to part."—"Apparently."

"Is the one itself part of itself?"—"In no way."—"So neither

could it be a whole in relation to itself as part of itself, because then it would be a part in relation to itself."—"No, it could
c not."—"But is the one different from one?"—"No indeed."—"So it couldn't be different from itself."—"Certainly not."—"So if it is neither different nor whole nor part in relation to itself, must it not then be the same as itself?"—"Necessarily."

"What about this? Must not that which is in something different from itself – the self that is in the same thing as itself – be different from itself, if in fact it is also to be in something different?"—"It seems so to me."—"In fact the one was shown to be so, since it is, at the same time, both in itself and in a different thing."—"Yes, it was."—"So in this way the one, as it
d seems, would be different from itself."—"So it seems."

"Now, if anything is different from something, won't it be different from something that is different?"—"Necessarily."— "Aren't all the things that are not-one different from the one, and the one from the things not-one?"—"Doubtless."—"Therefore the one would be different from the others."—"Different."

"Consider this: aren't the same itself and the different opposite to each other?"—"Doubtless."—"Then will the same ever consent to be in the different, or the different in the same?"—"It won't."—"So if the different is never to be in the same, there is no being that the different is in for any time; for if it were in
e anything for any time whatsoever, for that time the different would be in the same. Isn't that so?"—"Just so."—"But since it is never in the same, the different would never be in any being."— "True."—"So the different wouldn't be in the things not-one or in the one."—"Yes, you're quite right."—"So not by the different would the one be different from the things not-one or they different from it."—"No, it wouldn't."—"Nor by themselves would they be different from each other, if they don't partake
147 of the different."—"Obviously not."—"But if they aren't different by themselves or by the different, wouldn't they in fact entirely avoid being different from each other?"—"They would."—"But neither do the things not-one partake of the one; otherwise they would not be not-one, but somehow one."— "True."—"So the things not-one could not be a number either; for in that case, too, they would not be absolutely not-one, since they would at least have number."—"Yes, you're quite right."— "And again: are the things not-one parts of the one? Or would

the things not-one in that case, too, partake of the one?"—"They would."—"So if it is in every way one, and they are in every way not-one, the one would be neither a part of the things not-   *b* one nor a whole with them as parts; and, in turn, the things not-one would be neither parts of the one nor wholes in relation to the one as part."—"No, they wouldn't."—"But in fact we said that things that are neither parts nor wholes nor different from each other will be the same as each other."—"Yes, we did."— "So are we to say that the one, since it is so related to the things not-one, is the same as they are?"—"Let's say so."—"Therefore the one, as it seems, is both different from the others and itself, and the same as the others and itself."—"It certainly looks that way from our argument."

"Would the one then also be both like and unlike itself and   *c* the others?"—"Perhaps."—"At any rate, since it was shown to be different from the others, the others would surely also be different from it."—"To be sure."—"Wouldn't it be different from the others just as they are different from it, and neither more nor less?"—"Yes, why not?"—"So if neither more nor less, in like degree."—"Yes."—"Accordingly, insofar as it has the property of being different from the others and they, likewise, have the property of being different from it, in this way the one would have a property the same as the others, and they would have a property the same as it."—"What do you mean?"

"As follows: don't you apply to something each name you   *d* use?"—"I do."—"Now, could you use the same name either more than once or once?"—"I could."—"So if you use it once, do you call by name that thing whose name it is, but not that thing, if you use it many times? Or whether you utter the same name once or many times, do you quite necessarily always also speak of the same thing?"—"To be sure."—"Now 'different' in particular is a name for something, isn't it?"—"Certainly."—"So when you utter it, whether once or many times, you don't apply   *e* it to another thing or name something other than that thing whose name it is."—"Necessarily."—"Whenever we say 'the others are different from the one' and 'the one is different from the others,' although we use 'different' twice, we don't apply it to another nature, but always to that nature whose name it is."— "Of course."—"So insofar as the one is different from the others, and the others from the one, on the basis of having the property *148* difference itself, the one would have a property not other, but the same as the others. And that which has a property the same is surely like, isn't it?"—"Yes."—"Indeed, insofar as the one has the property of being different from the others, owing to that property itself it would be altogether like them all, because it is altogether different from them all."—"So it seems."

"Yet, on the other hand, the like is opposite to the unlike."—"Yes."—"Isn't the different also opposite to the same?"—"That too."—"But this was shown as well: that the one is the same as
b the others."—"Yes, it was."—"And being the same as the others is the property opposite to being different from the others."—"Certainly."—"Insofar as the one is different, it was shown to be like."—"Yes."—"So insofar as it is the same, it will be unlike, owing to the property opposite to that which makes it like. And surely the different made it like?"—"Yes."—"So the same will make it unlike; otherwise it won't be opposite to the different."—
c "So it seems."—"Therefore the one will be like and unlike the others – insofar as it is different, like, and insofar as it is the same, unlike."—"Yes, it admits of this argument too, as it seems."

"It also admits of the following."—"What is that?"—"Insofar as it has a property the same, it has a property that is not of another kind; and if it has a property that is not of another kind, it is not unlike; and if not unlike, it is like. But insofar as it has a property other, it has a property that is of another kind; and if it has a property that is of another kind, it is unlike."—"That's true."—"So because the one is the same as the others and because it is different, on both grounds and either, it would be
d both like and unlike the others."—"Certainly."

"So, in the same way, it will be like and unlike itself as well. Since in fact it was shown to be both different from itself and the same as itself, on both grounds and either, won't it be shown to be both like and unlike itself?"—"Necessarily."

"And what about this? Consider the question whether the one touches or does not touch itself and the others."—"Very well."—"Surely the one was shown to be in itself as a whole."—"That's right."—"Isn't the one also in the others?"—"Yes."—"Then inso-
e far as it is in the others, it would touch the others; but insofar as it is in itself, it would be kept from touching the others, and being in itself, would touch itself."—"Apparently."—"Thus the one would touch itself and the others."—"It would."

"And again, in this way: must not everything that is to touch something lie next to that which it is to touch, occupying the position adjacent to that occupied by what it touches?"—"Necessarily."—"So, too, the one, if it is to touch itself, must lie directly adjacent to itself, occupying a place next to that in which it itself is."—"Yes, it must."—"Now if the one were two it could do that and turn out to be in two places at the same time; but won't it *149* refuse as long as it is one?"—"Yes, you're quite right."—"So the same necessity that keeps the one from being two keeps it from touching itself."—"The same."

"But it won't touch the others either."—"Why?"—"Because, we say, that which is to touch must, while being separate, be next to what it is to touch, and there must be no third thing between them."—"True."—"So there must be at least two things if there is to be contact."—"There must."—"But if to the two items a third is added in a row, they themselves will be three, their contacts two."—"Yes."—"And thus whenever one item is *b* added, one contact is also added, and it follows that the contacts are always fewer by one than the multitude of the numbers. For in regard to the number being greater than the contacts, every later number exceeds all the contacts by an amount equal to that by which the first two exceeded their contacts, since thereafter one is added to the number and, at the same time, one contact *c* to the contacts."—"That's right."—"So however many the things are in number, the contacts are always fewer than they are by one."—"True."—"But if there is only one, and not two, there could not be contact."—"Obviously not."—"Certainly the things other than the one, we say, are not one and do not partake of it, if in fact they are other."—"No, they don't."—"So number is not in the others, if one is not in them."—"Obviously not."— "So the others are neither one nor two, nor do they have a name of any other number."—"No."—"So the one alone is one, and *d* there could not be two."—"Apparently not."—"So there is no contact, since there aren't two items."—"There isn't."—"Therefore, the one doesn't touch the others nor do the others touch the one, since in fact there is no contact."—"Yes, you're quite right."—"Thus, to sum up, the one both touches and does not touch the others and itself."—"So it seems."

"Is it then both equal and unequal to itself and the others?"— "How so?"—"If the one were greater or less than the others, or

e   they in turn greater or less than it, they wouldn't be in any way
greater or less than each other by the one being one and the
others being other than one – that is, by their own being – would
they? But if they each had equality in addition to their own
being, they would be equal to each other. And if the others had
largeness and the one had smallness, or vice versa, whichever
form had largeness attached would be greater, and whichever
had smallness attached would be less?"—"Necessarily."

"Then aren't there these two forms, largeness and smallness?
For certainly, if there weren't, they couldn't be opposite to each
other and couldn't occur in things that are."—"No. How could
150 they?"—"So if smallness occurs in the one, it would be either
in the whole of it or in part of it."—"Necessarily."—"What if it
were to occur in the whole? Wouldn't it be in the one either
by being stretched equally throughout the whole of it, or by
containing it?"—"Quite clearly."—"Wouldn't smallness, then,
if it were in the one equally throughout, be equal to it, but if
it contained the one, be larger?"—"Doubtless."—"So can
smallness be equal to or larger than something, and do the jobs
b   of largeness and equality, but not its own?"—"It can't."—"So
smallness could not be in the one as a whole; but if in fact it is
in the one, it would be in a part."—"Yes."—"But, again, not in
all the part. Otherwise, it will do exactly the same thing as it
did in relation to the whole: it will be equal to or larger than
whatever part it is in."—"Necessarily."—"Therefore smallness
will never be in any being, since it occurs neither in a part nor
in a whole. Nor will anything be small except smallness itself."—
"It seems not."

"So largeness won't be in the one either. For if it were, something else, apart from largeness itself, would be larger than some-
c   thing, namely, that which the largeness is in – and that too,
although there is for it no small thing, which it must exceed, if
in fact it is large. But this is impossible, since smallness is nowhere in anything."—"True."

"But largeness itself is not greater than anything other than
smallness itself, nor is smallness less than anything other than
largeness itself."—"No, they aren't."—"So the others aren't
greater than the one, nor are they less, because they have neither
largeness nor smallness. Nor do these two themselves – large-
d   ness and smallness – have, in relation to the one, their power

of exceeding and being exceeded; they have it, rather, in relation to each other. Nor could the one, in its turn, be greater or less than these two or the others, since it has neither largeness nor smallness."—"It certainly appears not."—"So if the one is neither greater nor less than the others, it must neither exceed them nor be exceeded by them?"—"Necessarily."—"Now, it is quite necessary that something that neither exceeds nor is exceeded be equally matched, and if equally matched, equal."—"No doubt."

"Furthermore, the one would also itself be so in relation to   e
itself: having neither largeness nor smallness in itself, it would neither be exceeded by nor exceed itself, but, being equally matched, would be equal to itself."—"Of course."—"Therefore the one would be equal to itself and the others."—"Apparently."

"And yet, since it is in itself, it would also be around itself on the outside, and as container it would be greater than itself, but as contained it would be less. And thus the one would be greater 151 and less than itself."—"Yes, it would be."

"Isn't this necessary too, that there be nothing outside the one and the others?"—"No doubt."—"But surely what is must always be somewhere."—"Yes."—"Then won't that which is in something be in something greater as something less? For there is no other way that something could be in something else."— "No, there isn't."—"Since there is nothing else apart from the others and the one, and since they must be in something, must they not in fact be in each other – the others in the one and the one in the others – or else be nowhere?"—"Apparently."—"So,   b
on the one hand, because the one is in the others, the others would be greater than the one, since they contain it, and the one would be less than the others, since it is contained. On the other hand, because the others are in the one, by the same argument the one would be greater than the others and they less than it."—"So it seems."—"Therefore the one is both equal to, and greater and less than, itself and the others."—"Apparently."

"And if in fact it is greater and less and equal, it would be of measures equal to, and more and fewer than, itself and the others; and since of measures, also of parts."—"Doubtless."—   c
"So, since it is of equal and more and fewer measures, it would also be fewer and more than itself and the others in number, and, correspondingly, equal to itself and the others."—"How

so?"—"It would surely be of more measures than those things it is greater than, and of as many parts as measures; and likewise it would be of fewer measures and parts than those things it is less than; and correspondingly for the things it is equal to."—"Just so."—"Since it is, then, greater and less than, and equal
d   to, itself, would it not be of measures more and fewer than, and equal to, itself? And since of measures, also of parts?"—"Doubtless."—"So, since it is of parts equal to itself, it would be equal to itself in multitude, but since it is of more and fewer parts, it would be more and fewer than itself in number."—"Apparently."—"Now won't the one be related in the same way also to the others? Because it appears larger than they, it must also be more than they are in number; and because it appears smaller, fewer; and because it appears equal in largeness, it must also be equal to the others in multitude."—"Necessarily."—
e   "Thus, in turn, as it seems, the one will be equal to, and more and fewer than, itself and the others in number."—"It will."

"Does the one also partake of time? And, in partaking of time, is it and does it come to be both younger and older than, and neither younger nor older than, itself and the others?"—"How so?"—"If in fact one is, being surely belongs to it."—"Yes."—"But is *to be* simply partaking of being with time present, just
152 as *was* is communion with being together with time past, and, in turn, *will be* is communion with being together with time future?"—"Yes, it is."—"So the one partakes of time, if in fact it partakes of being."—"Certainly."

"Of time advancing?"—"Yes."—"So the one always comes to be older than itself, if in fact it goes forward in step with time."—"Necessarily."—"Do we recall that the older comes to be older than something that comes to be younger?"—"We do."—"So, since the one comes to be older than itself, wouldn't it come to be older than a self that comes to be younger?"—"Necessarily."—
b   "Thus it indeed comes to be both younger and older than itself."—"Yes."

"But it *is* older, isn't it, whenever, in coming to be, it is at the now time, between *was* and *will be*? For as it proceeds from the past to the future, it certainly won't jump over the now."—"No, it won't."—"Doesn't it stop coming to be older when it
c   encounters the now? It doesn't come to be, but is then already older, isn't it? For if it were going forward, it could never be

grasped by the now. A thing going forward is able to lay hold of both the now and the later – releasing the now and reaching for the later, while coming to be between the two, the later and the now."—"True."—"But if nothing that comes to be can sidestep the now, whenever a thing *is* at this point, it always stops its coming-to-be and then is whatever it may have come d to be."—"Apparently."—"So, too, the one: whenever, in coming to be older, it encounters the now, it stops its coming-to-be and is then older."—"Of course."—"So it also is older than that very thing it was coming to be older than – and wasn't it coming to be older than itself?"—"Yes."—"And the older is older than a younger?"—"It is."—"So the one is then also younger than itself, whenever, in its coming-to-be older, it encounters the now."— "Necessarily."—"Yet the now is always present to the one throughout its being; for the one always is now, whenever it e is."—"No doubt."—"Therefore the one always both is and comes to be older and younger than itself."—"So it seems."

"Is it or does it come to be for more time than itself or an equal time?"—"An equal."—"But if it comes to be or is for an equal time, it is the same age."—"Doubtless."—"And that which is the same age is neither older nor younger."—"No, it isn't."— "So the one, since it comes to be and is for a time equal to itself, neither is nor comes to be younger or older than itself."—"I think not."

"And again: what of the others?"—"I can't say."— "This much, surely, you can say: things other than the one, if in fact 153 they are different things and not *a* different thing, are more than one. A different thing would be one, but different things are more than one and would have multitude."—"Yes, they would."— "And, being a multitude, they would partake of a greater number than the one."—"Doubtless."—"Now, shall we say in connection with number that things that are more or things that are less come to be and have come to be earlier?"—"Things that are less."—"So, the least thing first; and this is the one. Isn't that so?"—"Yes."—"So of all the things that have number the one b has come to be first. And the others, too, all have number, if in fact they are others and not an other."—"Yes, they do."—"But that which has come to be first, I take it, has come to be earlier, and the others later; and things that have come to be later are younger than what has come to be earlier. Thus the others would be younger than the one, and the one older than they."—"Yes, it would."

"What about the following? Could the one have come to be in a way contrary to its own nature, or is that impossible?"—

c   "Impossible."—"Yet the one was shown to have parts, and if parts, a beginning, an end, and a middle."—"Yes."—"Well, in the case of all things – the one itself and each of the others – doesn't a beginning come to be first, and after the beginning all the others up to the end?"—"To be sure."—"Furthermore, we shall say that all these others are parts of some one whole, but that it itself has come to be one and whole at the same time as the end."—"Yes, we shall."—"An end, I take it, comes to be

d   last, and the one naturally comes to be at the same time as it. And so if in fact the one itself must not come to be contrary to nature, it would naturally come to be later than the others, since it has come to be at the same time as the end."—"Apparently."— "Therefore the one is younger than the others, and the others are older than it."—"That, in turn, appears to me to be so."

"But again: must not a beginning or any other part of the one or of anything else, if in fact it is a part and not parts, be one, since it is *a* part?"—"Necessarily."—"Accordingly, the one would come to be at the same time as the first part that comes

e   to be, and at the same time as the second; and it is absent from none of the others that come to be – no matter what is added to what – until, upon arriving at the last part, it comes to be one whole, having been absent at the coming-to-be of neither the middle nor the first nor the last nor any other part."—"True."— "Therefore the one is the same age as all the others. And so, unless the one itself is naturally contrary to nature, it would have come to be neither earlier nor later than the others, but at

154 the same time. And according to this argument the one would be neither older nor younger than the others, nor the others older or younger than it. But according to our previous argument, it was both older and younger than they, and likewise they were both older and younger than it."—"Of course."

"That's how it is and has come to be. But what about its coming-to-be both older and younger, and neither older nor younger, than the others and they than it? Is the case with coming-to-be just as it is with being, or is it different?"—"I can't

b   say."—"But I can say this much, at least: if something is indeed

older than another thing, it could not come to be still older by
an amount greater than the original difference in age. Nor, in
turn, could the younger come to be still younger. For equals
added to unequals, in time or anything else at all, always make
them differ by an amount equal to that by which they differed
at first."—"No doubt."—"So what is older or younger could
never come to be older or younger than what is older or younger,   c
if in fact they always differ in age by an equal amount. On the
contrary, something is and has come to be older, and something
younger, but they do not come to be so."—"True."—"So also
the one, since it is older or younger, never comes to be older or
younger than the others that are older or younger than it."—
"Yes, you're quite right."

   "But consider whether it comes to be older and younger in
this way."—"In what way?"—"In the way that the one was
shown to be older than the others and they older than it."—
"What of that?"—"When the one is older than the others, it has
surely come to be for more time than they."—"Yes."—"Go back   d
and consider: if we add an equal time to more and less time,
will the more differ from the less by an equal or a smaller fraction?"[26]—"A smaller."—"So the one's difference in age in relation to the others will not be in the future just what it was at
first. On the contrary, by getting an increment of time equal to
the others, it will differ from them in age always less than it did
before. Isn't that so?"—"Yes."—"Wouldn't that which differs
from anything in age less than before come to be younger than   e
before in relation to those things it was previously older than?"—
"Younger."—"And if the one comes to be younger, don't those
others, in turn, come to be older than before in relation to it?"—
"Certainly."—"So what is younger comes to be older in relation
to what has come to be earlier and is older, but it never is older.
On the contrary, it always comes to be older than that thing.
For the older advances toward the younger, while the younger
advances toward the older. And, in the same way, the older, in   155
its turn, comes to be younger than the younger. For both, by
going toward their opposites, come to be each other's opposite,
the younger coming to be older than the older, and the older

---

26. The word translated here and below as "fraction" is *morion*. *Morion*
and *meros* are elsewhere translated as "part."

younger than the younger. But they could not come to *be* so.
For if they came to be, they would no longer *come* to be, but
would be so. But as it is they come to be older and younger than
each other. The one comes to be younger than the others, because
it was shown to be older and to have come to be earlier, whereas
b   the others come to be older than the one, because they have
come to be later.

"And by the same argument the others, too, come to be
younger in relation to the one, since in fact they were shown to
be older than it and to have come to be earlier."—"Yes, it does
appear so."

"Well then, insofar as nothing comes to be older or younger
than a different thing, owing to their always differing from each
other by an equal number, the one would not come to be older
or younger than the others, and they would not come to be older
or younger than it. But insofar as things that came to be earlier
must differ from things that come to be later by a fraction that
c   is always different, and vice versa, in this way they must come
to be older and younger than each other – both the others than
the one and the one than the others."—"Of course."—"To sum
up all this, the one itself both is and comes to be older and
younger than itself and the others, and it neither is nor comes
to be older or younger than itself or the others."—"Exactly."

"And since the one partakes of time and of coming to be older
d   and younger, must it not also partake of time past, future, and
present – if in fact it partakes of time?"—"Necessarily."—"Therefore, the one was and is and will be, and was coming to be
and comes to be and will come to be."—"To be sure."—"And
something could belong to it and be of it, in the past, present,
and future."—"Certainly."—"And indeed there would be
knowledge and opinion and perception of it, if in fact even now
we are engaging in all those activities concerning it."—"You're
right."—"And a name and an account belong to it, and it is
e   named and spoken of. And all such things as pertain to the
others also pertain to the one."—"That's exactly so."

Appendix to Deductions 1 and 2

"Let's speak of it yet a third time. If the one is as we have
described it – being both one and many and neither one nor

many, and partaking of time – must it not, because it is one, sometimes partake of being, and in turn because it is not, sometimes not partake of being?"—"Necessarily."—"When it partakes, can it at that time not partake, or partake when it doesn't?"—"It cannot."—"So it partakes at one time, and doesn't partake at another; for only in this way could it both partake and not partake of the same thing."—"That's right."—"Isn't there, then, a definite time when it gets a share of being and *156* when it parts from it? Or how can it at one time have and at another time not have the same thing, if it never gets and releases it?"—"In no way."

"Don't you in fact call getting a share of being 'coming-to-be'?"—"I do."—"And parting from being 'ceasing-to-be'?"—"Most certainly."—"Indeed the one, as it seems, when it gets and releases being, comes to be and ceases to be."—"Necessarily."—"And since it is one and many and comes to be and ceases to *b* be, doesn't its being many cease to be whenever it comes to be one, and doesn't its being one cease to be whenever it comes to be many?"—"Certainly."—"Whenever it comes to be one and many, must it not separate and combine?"—"It certainly must."—"Furthermore, whenever it comes to be like and unlike, must it not be made like and unlike?"—"Yes."—"And whenever it comes to be greater and less and equal, must it not increase and decrease and be made equal?"—"Just so."

"And whenever, being in motion, it comes to a rest, and *c* whenever, being at rest, it changes to moving, it must itself, presumably, be in no time at all."—"How is that?"—"It won't be able to undergo being previously at rest and later in motion or being previously in motion and later at rest without changing."—"Obviously not."—"Yet there is no time in which something can, simultaneously, be neither in motion nor at rest."—"Yes, you're quite right."—"Yet surely it also doesn't change without changing."—"Hardly."—"So when does it change? For it does not change while it is at rest or in motion, or while it is in time."—"Yes, you're quite right."

"Is there, then, this queer thing in which it might be, just *d* when it changes?"—"What queer thing?"—"The instant. The instant seems to signify something such that changing occurs from it to each of two states. For a thing doesn't change from rest while rest continues, or from motion while motion continues.

Rather, this queer creature, the instant, lurks between motion
e   and rest – being in no time at all – and to it and from it the
moving thing changes to resting and the resting thing changes
to moving."—"It looks that way."—"And the one, if in fact it
both rests and moves, could change to each state – for only in
this way could it do both. But in changing, it changes at an
instant, and when it changes, it would be in no time at all, and
just then it would be neither in motion nor at rest."—"No, it
wouldn't."

"Is it so with the other changes too? Whenever the one changes
157 from being to ceasing-to-be, or from not-being to coming-to-be,
isn't it then between certain states of motion and rest? And then
it neither is nor is not, and neither comes to be nor ceases to
be?"—"It seems so, at any rate."—"Indeed, according to the
same argument, when it goes from one to many and from many
to one, it is neither one nor many, and neither separates nor
combines. And when it goes from like to unlike and from unlike
to like, it is neither like nor unlike, nor is it being made like or
b   unlike. And when it goes from small to large and to equal and
vice versa, it is neither small nor large nor equal; nor would it
be increasing or decreasing or being made equal."—"It seems
not."—"The one, if it is, could undergo all that."—"Doubtless."

Deduction 3

"Must we not examine what the others would undergo, if one
is?"—"We must."—"Are we to say, then, what properties things
other than the one must have, if one is?"—"Let's do."—"Well
then, since in fact they are other than the one, the others are
not the one. For if they were, they would not be other than the
c   one."—"That's right."

"And yet the others are not absolutely deprived of the one,
but somehow partake of it."—"In what way?"—"In that things
other than the one are surely other because they have parts; for if
they didn't have parts, they would be altogether one."—"That's
right."—"And parts, we say, are parts of that which is a
whole."—"Yes, we do."—"Yet the whole of which the parts are
to be parts must be one thing composed of many, because each
of the parts must be part, not of many, but of a whole."—"Why
is that?"—"If something were to be part of many, in which it itself

is, it will, of course, be both part of itself, which is impossible, and   *d*
of each one of the others, if in fact it is part of all of them. For
if it is not part of one, it will be part of the others, that one
excepted, and thus it will not be part of each one. And if it is
not part of each, it will be part of none of the many. But if
something is part of none, it cannot be a part, or anything else
at all, of all those things of which it is no part of any."—"It
certainly appears so."—"So the part would not be part of many
things or all, but of some one character and of some one thing,
which we call a 'whole,' since it has come to be one complete   *e*
thing composed of all. This is what the part would be part of."—
"Absolutely."—"So if the others have parts, they would also
partake of some one whole."[27]—"Certainly."—"So things other
than the one must be one complete whole with parts."—
"Necessarily."

"Furthermore, the same account applies also to each part,
since it too must partake of the one. For if each of them is a   *158*
part, 'each,' of course, signifies that it is one thing, detached
from the others and being by itself, if in fact it is to be *each*."—
"That's right."—"But clearly it would partake of the one, while
being something other than one. Otherwise, it wouldn't partake,
but would itself be one. But as it is, it is surely impossible for
anything except the one itself to be one."—"Impossible."

"But both the whole and the part must partake of the one; for
the whole will be one thing of which the parts are parts, and in
turn each thing that is part of a whole will be one part of the
whole."—"Just so."—"Well, then, won't things that partake of   *b*
the one partake of it, while being different from it?"—"Doubtless."—"And things different from the one would surely be
many; for if things other than the one were neither one nor more
than one, they would be nothing."—"Yes, you're quite right."

"Since both things that partake of the oneness of a part and
things that partake of the oneness of a whole are more than one,
must not those things themselves that get a share of the one in
fact be unlimited in multitude?"—"How so?"—"Let's observe
the following: isn't it the case that, at the time when they get a

27. The Greek is *tou holou te kai henos*, which could also be translated
as "wholeness and oneness." The same phrase occurs at 153c6, where
that translation would be inappropriate.

share of the one, they get a share, while not being one and not partaking of the one?"—"Quite clearly."—"While being multi-

c   tudes, then, in which oneness is not present?"—"Certainly, multitudes."—"Now, if we should be willing to subtract, in thought, the very least we can from these multitudes, must not that which is subtracted, too, be a multitude and not one, if in fact it doesn't partake of the one?"—"Necessarily."—"So always, as we examine in this way its nature, itself by itself, different from the form, won't as much of it as we ever see be unlimited in multitude?"—"Absolutely."

"Furthermore, whenever each part comes to be one part, the
d   parts then have a limit in relation to each other and in relation to the whole, and the whole has a limit in relation to the parts."—"Quite so."—"Accordingly, it follows for things other than the one that from the one and themselves gaining communion with each other, as it seems, something different comes to be in them, which affords a limit for them in relation to each other; but their own nature, by themselves, affords unlimitedness."—"Apparently."—"In this way, indeed, things other than the one, taken both as wholes and part by part, both are unlimited and partake of a limit."—"Certainly."

e   "Well, aren't they both like and unlike each other and themselves?"—"In what way?"—"On the one hand, insofar as they are all unlimited by their own nature, they would in this way have a property the same."—"Certainly."—"Furthermore, insofar as they all partake of a limit, in this way, too, they would all have a property the same."—"Doubtless."—"On the other hand, insofar as they are both limited and unlimited, they have these properties, which are opposite to each other."—"Yes."—
159   "And opposite properties are as unlike as possible."—"To be sure."—"So in respect of either property they would be like themselves and each other, but in respect of both properties they would be utterly opposite and unlike both themselves and each other."—"It looks that way."—"Thus the others would be both like and unlike themselves and each other."—"Just so."

"And indeed we will have no further trouble in finding that things other than the one are both the same as and different from each other, both in motion and at rest, and have all the opposite properties, since in fact they were shown to have those
b   we mentioned."—"You're right."

Deduction 4

"Well, then, suppose we now concede those results as evident and examine again, if one is: Are things other than the one also not so, or only so?"—"Of course."—"Let's say from the beginning, what properties things other than the one must have, if one is."—"Yes, let's do."—"Must not the one be separate from the others, and the others separate from the one?"—"Why?"— "Because surely there is not something else in addition to them that is both other than the one and other than the others; for all things have been mentioned, once the one and the others are   c mentioned."—"Yes, all things."—"So there is no further thing, different from them, in which same thing the one and the others could be."—"No, there isn't."—"So the one and the others are never in the same thing."—"It seems not."—"So they are separate?"—"Yes."

"Furthermore, we say that what is really one doesn't have parts."—"Obviously not."—"So the one could not be in the others as a whole, nor could parts of it be in them, if it is separate from the others and doesn't have parts."—"Obviously not."— "So the others could in no way partake of the one, if they partake   d neither by getting some part of it nor by getting it as a whole."— "It seems not."—"In no way, then, are the others one, nor do they have any oneness in them."—"Yes, you're quite right."

"So the others aren't many either; for each of them would be one part of a whole, if they were many. But as it is, things other than the one are neither one nor many nor a whole nor parts, since they in no way partake of the one."—"That's right."— "Therefore, the others are not themselves two or three, nor are two or three in them, if in fact they are entirely deprived of the   e one."—"Just so."

"So the others aren't themselves like and unlike the one, and likeness and unlikeness aren't in them. For if they were themselves like and unlike, or had likeness and unlikeness in them, things other than the one would surely have in themselves two forms opposite to each other."—"Apparently."—"But it was impossible for things that couldn't partake even of one to partake of any two."—"Impossible."—"So the others are neither like nor unlike nor both. If they were like or unlike, they would partake   160 of one of the two forms, and if they were both, they would partake of two opposite forms. But these alternatives were shown to be impossible."—"True."

"So they are neither the same nor different, neither in motion nor at rest, neither coming to be nor ceasing to be, neither greater nor less nor equal. Nor do they have any other such properties. For if the others submit to having any such property, they will partake of one and two and three and odd and even, of which *b* it was shown they could not partake, since they are in every way entirely deprived of the one."—"Very true."

"Thus if one is, the one is all things and is not even one, both in relation to itself and, likewise, in relation to the others."— "Exactly."

Deduction 5

"So far so good. But must we not next examine what the consequences must be, if the one is not?"—"Yes, we must."—"What, then, would this hypothesis be: 'if one is not'? Does it differ at all from this hypothesis: 'if not-one is not'?"—"Of course it differs."—"Does it merely differ, or is saying 'if not-one is not' *c* the complete opposite of saying, 'if one is not'?"—"The complete opposite."—"What if someone were to say, 'if largeness is not' or 'if smallness is not' or anything else like that, would it be clear in each case that what he is saying is not is something different?"—"Certainly."—"So now, too, whenever he says, 'if one is not,' isn't it clear that what he says is not is different from the others, and don't we recognize what he means?"— "We do."—"So he speaks of something, in the first place, knowable, and in the second, different from the others, whenever he says 'one,' whether he attaches being or not-being to it; for we *d* still know what thing is said not to be, and that it is different from the others. Isn't that so?"—"Necessarily."

"Then we must state from the beginning as follows what must be the case, if one is not. First, as it seems, this must be so for it, that there is knowledge of it; otherwise we don't even know what is meant when someone says, 'if one is not'."—"True."— "And it must be the case that the others are different from it – or else it isn't said to be different from them?"—"Certainly."— "Therefore difference in kind pertains to it in addition to knowl- *e* edge. For someone doesn't speak of the difference in kind of the others when he says that the one is different from the others, but of *that* thing's difference in kind."—"Apparently."

"Furthermore, the one that is not partakes of *that* and of *something, this, to this, these,* and so on; for the one could not be mentioned, nor could things be different from the one, nor could anything belong to it or be of it, nor could it be said to be anything, unless it had a share of *something* and the rest."— "That's right."—"The one can't *be,* if in fact it is not, but nothing prevents it from partaking of many things. Indeed, it's even necessary, if in fact it's that one and not another that is not. If, 161 however, neither the one nor *that* is not to be, but the account is about something else, we shouldn't even utter a sound. But if that one and not another is posited not to be, it must have a share of *that* and of many other things."—"Quite certainly."

"So it has unlikeness, too, in relation to the others. For things other than the one, since they are different, would also be different in kind."—"Yes."—"And aren't things different in kind other in kind?"—"Doubtless."—"Aren't things other in kind un-like?"—"Unlike, certainly."—"Well, then, if in fact they are un- *b* like the one, clearly things unlike would be unlike an unlike."— "Clearly."—"So the one would also have unlikeness, in relation to which the others are unlike it."—"So it seems."

"But, then, if it has unlikeness to the others, must it not have likeness to itself?"—"How so?"—"If the one has unlikeness to one, the argument would surely not be about something of the same kind as the one, nor would the hypothesis be about one, but about something other than one."—"Certainly."—"But it must not be."—"No indeed."—"Therefore the one must have *c* likeness of itself to itself."—"It must."

"Furthermore, it is not equal to the others either; for if it were equal, it would then both be, and be like them in respect of equality. But those are both impossible, if in fact one is not."— "Impossible."—"Since it is not equal to the others, must not the others, too, be not equal to it?"—"Necessarily."—"Aren't things that are not equal unequal?"—"Yes."—"And aren't things un-equal unequal to something unequal?"—"Doubtless."—"So the one partakes also of inequality, in relation to which the others *d* are unequal to it."—"It does."

"But largeness and smallness are constitutive of inequality."— "Yes, they are."—"So do largeness and smallness, too, belong to this one?"—"It looks that way."—"Yet largeness and smallness always stand apart from each other."—"Certainly."—"So there is always something between them."—"There is."—"Then can you mention anything between them other than equality?"—"No, just that."—"Therefore whatever has largeness and smallness also has equality, since it is between them."—"Apparently."—"The one, if it is not, would have, as it seems, a share of equality, largeness, and smallness."—"So it seems."

"Furthermore, it must also somehow partake of being."—"How is that?"—"It must be in the state we describe; for if it is not so, we wouldn't speak truly when we say that the one is not. But if we do speak truly, it is clear that we say things that are. Isn't that so?"—"It is indeed so."—"And since we claim to speak truly, we must claim also to speak of things that are."—"Necessarily."—"Therefore, as it seems, the one *is* a not-being; for if it is not to *be* a not-being, but is somehow to give up its being in relation to not-being, it will straightway be a being."—"Absolutely."—"So if it is not to be, it must have *being* a not-being as a bond in regard to its not-being, just as, in like manner, what is must have *not-being* what is not, in order that it, in its turn, may completely be.[28] This is how what is would most of all be and what is not would not be: on the one hand, by what is, if it is completely to be, partaking of being in regard to being a being and of not-being in regard to being a not-being; and, on the other hand, by what is not, if in its turn what is not is completely not to be, partaking of not-being in regard to not-being a not-being and of being in regard to being a not-being."[29]—"Very true."—"Accordingly, since in fact what is has a share of not-being and what is not has a share of being, so, too, the one, since it is not, must have a share of being in regard to its not-being."—"Necessarily."—"Then the one, if it is not, appears also to have being."—"Apparently."—"And of course not-being, if in fact it is not."—"Doubtless."

"Can something that is in some state not be so, without changing from that state?"—"It cannot."—"So everything of the sort

_e_

162

_b_

---

28. We have accepted Shorey's deletion of *einai* at 162a6.

29. We have followed the manuscript readings printed in the text of the Budé edition by Diès 1923. The Oxford text follows Shorey in deleting a negative at 162b2 and inserting it at 162a8.

we've described, which is both so and not so, signifies a   *c*
change."—"Doubtless."—"And a change is a motion – or what
shall we call it?"—"A motion."—"Now wasn't the one shown
both to be and not to be?"—"Yes."—"Therefore, it appears both
to be so and not so."—"So it seems."—"Therefore the one that
is not has been shown also to move, since in fact it has been
shown to change from being to not-being."—"It looks that way."

"Yet, on the other hand, if it is nowhere among the things
that are – as it isn't, if in fact it is not – it couldn't travel from
one place to another."—"Obviously not."—"So it couldn't move
by switching place."—"No, it couldn't."—"Nor could it rotate   *d*
in the same thing, because it nowhere touches the same thing.
For that which is the same is a being, and what is not cannot
be in anything that is."—"No, it can't."—"Therefore the one, if
it is not, would be unable to rotate in that in which it is not."—
"Yes, you're quite right."—"And, surely, the one isn't altered
from itself either, whether as something that is or as something
that is not. For the argument would no longer be about the one,
but about something else, if in fact the one were altered from
itself."—"That's right."—"But if it isn't altered and doesn't rotate in the same thing or switch place, could it still move somehow?"—"Obviously not."—"Yet what is unmoved must enjoy   *e*
repose, and what reposes must be at rest."—"Necessarily."—
"Therefore the one, as it seems, since it is not, is both at rest
and in motion."—"So it seems."

"Furthermore, if in fact it moves, it certainly must be altered;
for however something is moved, by just so much it is no longer   *163*
in the same state as it was, but in a different state."—"Just so."—
"Then because it moves, the one is also altered."—"Yes."—"And
yet, because it in no way moves, it could in no way be altered."—
"No, it couldn't."—"So insofar as the one that is not moves, it
is altered, but insofar as it doesn't move, it is not altered."—
"No, it isn't.—"Therefore the one, if it is not, is both altered and
not altered."—"Apparently."

"Must not that which is altered come to be different from what
it was before, and cease to be in its previous state; and must not
that which is not altered neither come to be nor cease to be?"—   *b*
"Necessarily."—"Therefore also the one, if it is not, comes to be
and ceases to be, if it is altered, and does not come to be or
cease to be, if it is not altered. And thus the one, if it is not,

both comes to be and ceases to be, and does not come to be or cease to be."—"Yes, you're quite right."

Deduction 6

"Let's go back again to the beginning to see whether things will appear the same to us as they do now, or different."—"Indeed, we must."—"Aren't we saying, if one is not, what the consequences must be for it?"—"Yes."—"When we say 'is not,' the words don't signify anything other than absence of being for whatever we say is not, do they?"—"Nothing other."—"When we say that something is not, are we saying that in a way it is not, but in a way it is? Or does this 'is not' signify without qualification that what is not is in no way at all and does not in any way partake of being?"—"Absolutely without qualification."—"Therefore what is not could neither be nor partake of being in any other way at all."—"No, it couldn't."

"Can coming-to-be and ceasing-to-be possibly be anything other than getting a share of being and losing it?"—"Nothing other."—"But what has no share of being could neither get nor lose it."—"Obviously not."—"So the one, since it in no way is, must in no way have, release, or get a share of, being."—"That's reasonable."—"So the one that is not neither ceases to be nor comes to be, since in fact it in no way partakes of being."—"Apparently not."—"So it also isn't altered in any way. For if it were to undergo this, it would then come to be and cease to be."—"True."—"And if it isn't altered, it must not move either?"—"Necessarily."—"And surely we won't say that what in no way is is at rest, since what is at rest must always be in some same thing."—"In the same thing, no doubt."—"Thus, let's say that what is not is, in turn, never at rest or in motion."—"Yes, you're quite right."

"But in fact nothing that is belongs to it; for then, by partaking of that, it would partake of being."—"Clearly."—"So neither largeness nor smallness nor equality belongs to it."—"No, they don't."—"Furthermore, it would have neither likeness nor difference in kind in relation to itself or in relation to the others."—"Apparently not."

"What about this? Can the others be related to it, if, necessarily, nothing belongs to it?"—"They can't."—"So the others are neither like nor unlike it, and they are neither the same as nor different from it."—"No, they aren't."—"And again: will *of that, to that, something, this, of this, of another, to another,* or time past, hereafter, or now, or knowledge, opinion, perception, an ac- *b* count, a name, or anything else that is be applicable to what is not?"—"It will not."—"Thus one, since it is not, is not in any state at all."—"At any rate, it certainly seems to be in no state at all."

Deduction 7

"Let's go on and say what properties the others must have, if one is not."—"Yes, let's do."—"They must surely be other; for if they weren't even other, we wouldn't be talking about the others."—"Just so."—"But if the argument is about the others, the others are different. Or don't you apply the names 'other' and 'different' to the same thing?"—"I do."—"And surely we *c* say that the different is different from a different thing, and the other is other than another thing?"—"Yes."—"So the others, too, if they are to be other, have something they will be other than."—"Necessarily."—"What would it be then? For they won't be other than the one, if it is indeed not."—"No, they won't."— "So they are other than each other, since that alternative remains for them, or else to be other than nothing."—"That's right."

"So they each are other than each other as multitudes; for they couldn't be so as ones, if one is not. But each mass of them, as it seems, is unlimited in multitude, and if you take what seems *d* to be smallest, in an instant, just as in a dream, instead of seeming to be one, it appears many, and instead of very small, immense in relation to the bits chopped from it."—"That's quite right."— "The others would be other than each other as masses of this sort, if they are other, and if one is not."—"Quite so."

"Well then, won't there be many masses, each appearing, but not being, one, if in fact one is not to be?"—"Just so."—"And there will seem to be a number of them, if in fact each seems to be one, although being many."—"Certainly."—"And among *e* them some appear even and some odd, although not really being so, if in fact one is not to be."—"Yes, you're quite right."

"Furthermore, a smallest too, we say, will seem to be among them; but this appears many and large in relation to each of

165 its many, because they are small."—"Doubtless."—"And each
mass will be conceived to be equal to its many small bits. For it
could not, in appearance, shift from greater to less, until it seems
to come to the state in between, and this would be an appearance
of equality."—"That's reasonable."

"Now won't it appear to have a limit in relation to another
mass, but itself to have no beginning, limit, or middle in relation
to itself?"—"Why is that?"—"Because whenever you grasp any
bit of them in thought as being a beginning, middle, or end,
b before the beginning another beginning always appears, and
after the end a different end is left behind, and in the middle
others more in the middle than the middle but smaller, because
you can't grasp each of them as one, since the one is not."—
"Very true."—"So every being that you grasp in thought must,
I take it, be chopped up and dispersed, because surely, without
oneness, it would always be grasped as a mass."—"Of
course."—"So must not such a thing appear one to a person
c dimly observing from far off; but to a person considering it keenly
from up close, must not each one appear unlimited in multitude,
if in fact it is deprived of the one, if it is not?"—"Indeed, most
necessarily."—"Thus the others must each appear unlimited and
as having a limit, and one and many, if one is not, but things
other than the one are."—"Yes, they must."

"Won't they also seem to be both like and unlike?"—"Why is
that?"—"Just as, to someone standing at a distance, all things
in a painting,[30] appearing one, appear to have a property the
d same and to be like."—"Certainly."—"But when the person
comes closer, they appear many and different and, by the appearance of the different, different in kind and unlike themselves."—
"Just so."—"So the masses must also appear both like and unlike
themselves and each other."—"Of course."

"Accordingly, if one is not and many are, the many must
appear both the same as and different from each other, both in
contact and separate from themselves, both moving with every
motion and in every way at rest, both coming to be and ceasing
to be and neither, and surely everything of that sort, which it

---

30. Plato's word here refers specifically to painting that aims at the
illusion of volume through the contrast of light and shadow.

would now be easy enough for us to go through."—"Very true   *e*
indeed."

Deduction 8

"Let's go back to the beginning once more and say what must
be the case, if one is not, but things other than the one are."—
"Yes, let's do."—"Well, the others won't be one."—"Obviously
not."—"And surely they won't be many either, since oneness
would also be present in things that are many. For if none of
them is one, they are all nothing – so they also couldn't be
many."—"True."—"If oneness isn't present in the others, the
others are neither many nor one."—"No, they aren't."

"Nor even do they appear one or many."—"Why?"—"Because
the others have no communion in any way at all with any of   *166*
the things that are not, and none of the things that are not
belongs to any of the others, since things that are not have no
part."—"True."—"So no opinion or any appearance of what is
not belongs to the others, nor is not-being conceived in any way
at all in the case of the others."—"Yes, you're quite right."—
"So if one is not, none of the others is conceived to be one or
many, since, without oneness, it is impossible to conceive of   *b*
many."—"Yes, impossible."—"Therefore, if one is not, the others neither are nor are conceived to be one or many."—"It seems
not."

"So they aren't like or unlike either."—"No, they aren't."—
"And indeed, they are neither the same nor different, neither
in contact nor separate, nor anything else that they appeared to
be in the argument we went through before. The others neither
are nor appear to be any of those things, if one is not."—
"True."—"Then if we were to say, to sum up, 'if one is not,   *c*
nothing is,' wouldn't we speak correctly?"—"Absolutely."

"Let us then say this – and also that, as it seems, whether one
is or is not, it and the others both are and are not, and both
appear and do not appear all things in all ways, both in relation
to themselves and in relation to each other."—"Very true."